ABORTION AND THE WAYS
WE VALUE HUMAN LIFE

ABORTION AND THE WAYS WE VALUE HUMAN LIFE

Jeffrey Reiman

ROWMAN & LITTLEFIELD PUBLISHERS, INC.
Lanham • Boulder • New York • Oxford

ROWMAN & LITTLEFIELD PUBLISHERS, INC.

Published in the United States of America
by Rowman & Littlefield Publishers, Inc.
4720 Boston Way, Lanham, Maryland 20706

12 Hid's Copse Road
Cumnor Hill, Oxford OX2 9JJ, England

British Library Cataloguing in Publication Information Available

Library of Congress Cataloging-in-Publication Data
Reiman, Jeffrey H.
    Abortion and the ways we value human life / Jeffrey Reiman.
    p.   cm.
    Includes bibliographical references and index.
    ISBN 0-8476-9207-8 (cloth : alk. paper).—ISBN 0-8476-9208-6
(pbk. : alk. paper)
    1. Abortion—Moral and ethical aspects.   2. Fetus.   3. Life.
I. Title.
HQ767.15.R45   1999
363.46—dc21   98-39537
                                                              CIP

Printed in the United States of America

∞ ™ The paper used in this publication meets the minimum requirements of
American National Standard for Information Sciences—Permanence of Paper
for Printed Library Materials, ANSI Z39.48–1984.

for Sue

Contents

Preface and Acknowledgments

Not since slavery has a moral issue so divided Americans the way abortion does. About a million and a half American women have their pregnancies aborted each year. For some people, this is a sign of women's emergence into full citizenship, with full rights over themselves, their bodies, and their sexuality. For others, it is nothing less than a holocaust, a mass slaughter of innocents carried out with the legal endorsement of the state. Philosophers have done a great deal to clarify the moral questions surrounding abortion and yet they seem to have done very little toward healing this division. I add my contribution because I think that I have found a way to determine the morality of abortion that has been overlooked.

The special way in which we value human life when we think it is murder to kill human beings turns out to have a very distinctive shape, such that few considerations can account for it—few enough to eliminate all but one. When we think it is murder to kill a human being, we are valuing that particular individual's life, not human life in general. If we valued human life in general, or the good traits of human beings for that matter, we would have to think that murdering one person and replacing him with another would produce no loss. But we don't think that. We think that the loss of a particular human being is a loss that cannot be made up for by replacing that one with another one. Any account of this must be based on human beings' conscious awareness of their own individual lives—because nothing else provides rational grounds for valuing particular individuals against replacement. Consequently, I shall argue that our practice of morally condemning murder can only make sense as, in effect, a joint commitment to protect humans who have become conscious of their own lives against the loss of those lives. This leads to a very liberal solution to the abortion problem, and requires that the wrongness of infanticide be given a different basis than the wrongness of killing children and adults. I shall argue

ix

Preface and Acknowledgments

for both of these outcomes, and set that argument in the framework of a general theory of the ways in which we value human life at its various stages, from conception to death.

Many people have helped me in the thinking, research, and writing that went into this book, and I owe them all debts of gratitude. Emily Chiariello served as my research assistant during the academic year 1997–98 and assembled, organized, and annotated much of the historical, legal, and philosophical literature upon which the book is based. The first chapter of the book, on the history of attitudes and laws about abortion in the West, was read and commented on by Michael Kazin, Terence Murphy, Jamin Raskin, and Ira Robbins. I especially salute Terry Murphy for the generous spirit in which he helped me though he passionately disagrees with the conclusion that I defend. Susan Dwyer, Phillip Scribner, and David Luban read versions of the whole manuscript and gave me detailed comments and suggestions on it. I owe a special debt to David Luban since he encouraged me to work on the argument that I defend in this book after hearing an early form of it presented at the University of Maryland nearly ten years ago. I thank also Judith Copeland for a superb job of editing the manuscript, and Julie Kirsch of Rowman & Littlefield for guiding the book from typescript to publication. All of these individuals contributed to making this a better book than I could have written on my own.

I dedicate the book to my wife Sue Headlee for letting her spirit and idealism rub off on me. She always wanted me to write this book and she persuaded me to dare to hope that it might do some good.

Introduction

The Asymmetric Value of Human Life

A powerful clue to the solution of the moral problem of abortion has been largely ignored. I call it the *asymmetric value of human life*. This value, which we commonly attribute to human beings when we think it is morally wrong to kill them, is so unusual that it points us to the solution to the moral problem of abortion, as the shape of a keyhole points us to the key that will open it.

Argument

Let us assume what all pro-lifers and many pro-choicers believe, namely, that the fetus living inside a pregnant woman is a human being, at least in the biological sense. We can think of the normal career of such a (biological) human being as stretching from conception through the stages of pregnancy to birth and beyond into childhood and adulthood. Both pro-lifers and pro-choicers agree that, somewhere along this career, killing this human being (in the absence of excusing conditions, such as self-defense, war, legitimate punishment, or ignorance, insanity, duress, and so on) is *murder*. I use this term in a strictly moral, not legal, sense. Morally speaking, murder is the gravely immoral killing of a human being, whether or not it meets the specific legal criteria for criminal homicide. Pro-choicers and pro-lifers, then, disagree on when the killing of a biological human being is murder— but they agree that at some point it is.

Let us focus on this agreement: At some point, it is morally murder to kill a human being. Now, whenever we think it is murder to kill a human being, we are valuing human life in a special way. We can see the "shape" of this special valuing by considering the judgments that it normally implies: For example, though murder is gravely immoral, it is not immoral, at least not seriously immoral, to refuse to procreate.

Nor can the immorality of murder be made up for or canceled out if the killer adds another human being to the human population.

What these judgments reveal is that when we think it is morally murder to kill a human being, we are not simply valuing human life as such. If human life were valued as such, then there would be no net loss in value if one human being were killed and replaced with another, or there would be just as much loss from not procreating as from murder. So, murder could be made up for—its evil canceled out—by adding a new life to the population, and intentional contraception or abstinence by fertile couples would be as great an evil as murder—or murder would be as little an evil as contraception or abstinence. Such valuing, so to speak, values existing life and future possible life alike, or, as I shall say, *symmetrically*.[1]

Since we do not think that murder can be made up for by replacing the victim with another or that refusal to procreate is as great an evil as murder, it is evident that the valuing that underlies our views about the wrongness of murder is not symmetrical valuing. It is not a valuing of human life as such. Rather, it is a valuing of existing particular human lives *asymmetrically*, that is, far above the value of the lives of possible future human beings.

That we (pro-lifers and pro-choicers included) value human life or lives asymmetrically is a clue that can lead us to a solution to the moral problem of abortion. This clue works because asymmetric valuing is unusual enough to rule out a large number of common bases for valuing human life. Usually that we value something is about equally a reason for creating new ones and a reason for not destroying existing ones. This is not just a description of our conventional valuing practice. It is that, but it is also a claim about the nature of value itself. Normally, when we value something, we think this thing is good, and its goodness exercises a pull on our rational judgments and actions in all temporal directions. The goodness of something is roughly equally a reason for preserving existing ones and for producing new ones. Thus the normal way we value things is symmetric between existing ones and future ones. Such valuing will imply that killing one human and replacing her with a new one yields no net loss in value and that refusing

---

1. Of course, most of us do value human life in this way. This gives us a good reason to want to reproduce the human race—perhaps even a duty to do so. However, unless we are thought to be morally required to produce as many new human beings as we physically can (which no serious moral view recommends), the value of human life as such is a reason only for maintaining some optimal number of human beings alive. Since the optimal number can be maintained even though some are killed and replaced, this way of valuing human life cannot account for the way in which we think murder is immoral.

to procreate deprives the world of as much value as does killing. To account for the valuing of life that underlies our common beliefs about the wrongness of murder, then, we need to find a reasonable way of valuing human life asymmetrically.

It is no solution to this problem to say that human life has intrinsic worth, or that human beings are ends-in-themselves, and therefore human life has asymmetric value. That merely asserts that human life has asymmetric value; it does not show that it does or explain how it even could. Moreover, though I speak roughly about how much value the world is deprived of by killing one human and replacing her with another, or by killing versus refusing to procreate, my argument is in no way limited to a utilitarian ethical framework or even to one that thinks of value as quantifiable or maximizable. For example, a deontologist may think that killing a human is worse than refusing to procreate because killing is a greater violation of duty, and a virtue-ethicist may think that killing is worse because it manifests a more evil character.[2] However, both kinds of theorist will have to explain why killing a human is a greater violation of duty or manifests a worse character than refusing to procreate, *when both acts result in there being one less human being.* Thus, both kinds of moral theorists will have to find a reasonable way of valuing human life asymmetrically. It is this problem, which I believe haunts all moral approaches, that I am trying to speak of generally in terms of value added or taken from the world. So as not to have to continually translate this into the specific lingo of each moral approach, I ask the reader to keep in mind this larger purpose.

If we value human life by imputing goodness or intrinsic value to human beings because of their distinctive properties—rationality, creativity, capacity for loving attachment, and the like—such valuing is symmetric. It implies that one human with these properties could be killed and replaced without loss. Some may object that, even if we value something because of the goodness of its properties, our valuation need not imply that the valued one could acceptably be replaced by another with similar properties. For example, though you value Van Gogh's painting *Wheat Field with Crows* for its properties—its fantastic color, its careful composition, its overwhelming sense of foreboding,

---

2. A *utilitarian ethic* is one that aims at the maximization of some good, normally, happiness. A *deontologist* is a moral theorist who stresses duty or right conduct over the maximization of any good. A *virtue-ethicist* is a moral theorist who stresses the goodness of character over duty, right conduct, or the maximization of any good. The most important of utilitarian moral theorists are Jeremy Bentham and John Stuart Mill. The most important deontologist is Immanuel Kant. The most important virtue-ethicist is Aristotle. All of these approaches have contemporary representatives.

you would nevertheless object to someone destroying *Crows* and replacing it with another painting with equally impressive color, composition, and foreboding.[3]

This suggestion allows us to say more precisely what asymmetric valuing is by comparing a close look-alike. Note, to start, that we would object to the destruction of *Crows*, not because of properties that it shares with all paintings, but because of the very special constellation of properties that makes it a special painting. But nothing like this can be the basis of the value of human life, since that value is attributed to human beings generally, not just to special ones. I suspect that just about anything we value because of its properties and that we think is irreplaceable will have a similar specialness and thus not correspond to the way we value human beings. But, more importantly, even in such special cases, we are still not valuing asymmetrically. To see this, suppose that it was Van Gogh himself who destroyed *Crows*, and who then painted an identical duplicate as a replacement— so that the same special constellation of properties was present in the new painting. Surely there would be no loss of value when the first *Crows* was replaced by the second.

Compare this to the way in which we think about human beings. When we think it is gravely immoral to kill a human being, we think it would remain gravely immoral even if that human being were replaced by an identical duplicate with all the properties of the first one. *That is asymmetric valuing.* And, although, for it to have a rational foundation, asymmetric valuing will have to be based on some special properties of human beings, it cannot be based on imputing goodness to those properties (or to their possessors), since that is symmetric valuing: It implies the goodness of both existing and future possible human beings with those properties.

Since imputing goodness or intrinsic value to human traits (or to humans because of their traits) is not asymmetric valuing, I will argue that the object of asymmetric valuing must be human beings' own subjective awareness of, and caring about, their own lives. Note, as a first step toward understanding this claim, that, unlike traits like rationality, which in principle is as much a reason for valuing existing as future rational humans, human beings' conscious caring about their own lives pertains only to the particular lives that are theirs. This gives us, so to speak, a foot in the asymmetric door. Conscious beings care about their particular lives asymmetrically. Their caring about their own lives does not imply that it would be about equally good to preserve them as to

---

3. I owe this example to David Luban, who has pushed me hard and helpfully to clarify and defend my claims about the nature of valuing.

produce new beings, or equally bad to murder them as not to procreate. For them, nothing is comparable to the loss of the particular lives they care about.

However, this is only part of the story. Since it is we who are valuing human beings when we think it seriously immoral to kill them, *we* must be valuing consciously caring beings in a way that implies the asymmetric wrongness of killing them. Thus, our valuing cannot take the form of imputing goodness to consciously cared about lives. Such valuing is symmetric; it implies that we think that one cared about life is about as good as any other, even a future one.

To arrive at the asymmetric valuing of human life, then, we must value consciously cared about lives in a distinctive way. Instead of imputing goodness to consciously cared about lives, we must, I contend, value *that beings who consciously care about the continuation of their lives get what they care about.* This is an asymmetric way of valuing human life. We can value life in this way without thinking it good that there be, or come into existence, beings who care about their lives continuing, much as we can value that starving beings get fed without thinking it good that starving beings come into existence. Such valuing does not imply that it would be about equally good to create new beings as to preserve existing ones, since what we are valuing is that existing caring be satisfied. Nor does it imply that new caring beings should be brought into existence, for it implies nothing about whether it is better to care and be satisfied than never to have cared at all. Of course, I believe that it is almost always better to care and be satisfied than never to have cared at all. But that is a separate judgment. As long as this judgment is not implied by "valuing that caring beings get what they care about," the latter is an asymmetric way of valuing human life.

This much shows how we *can* value human life asymmetrically. But, if we are to account for asymmetric valuing as more than an irrational quirk, we must also see how it is *reasonable* to value life this way. Valuing that individuals who consciously care about the continuation of their lives get to continue is reasonable because, once conscious caring has come on the scene, the ending of the life that is cared about causes a loss that cannot be made good by replacing that life with another. Though this is a loss to a conscious being, I am not talking about a conscious loss, such as the anguish of a person who knows that he is about to die. Rather, once self-consciousness begins, our cares, desires, and reasons attach themselves to the ongoing "point of view" that constitutes our self, and that continues as our self even during periods of sleep or unconsciousness. It is the loss to this self—with or without consciousness of the loss or its approach—that I have in mind here. (You don't have to be aware of a loss to suffer it: If your house burned down while you were away, you underwent a loss at that very moment even if you didn't learn about the fire until your return.) This does not, however, amount to saying that there can be a loss to a being who is never conscious of her cares and desires. Rather, once conscious cares and desires come on the scene, they become abiding properties of the individual's self, against which a disappointment counts as a loss.

The loss of life to a being who has begun to care about living on cannot be made up for or made good by replacing the dead being with a new one. Consequently, to value that beings vulnerable to this loss be protected against suffering it implies that we believe that ending a life is far worse than not creating a new one, and thus it implies the asymmetric value of human life. But the only kind of being who can suffer this loss is a conscious being. For us to value life in a way that implies the appropriateness of protecting it against this loss, we must value *that* a consciously valuing being gets what she values. In a wide sense of the term, we can think of this kind of valuing as a form of *respect* because respect is a kind of indirect valuing, a valuing of another's valuing. Wrote Kant, "When I observe the duty of respect, I . . . keep myself within my own bounds in order not to deprive another of any of the value which he as a human being is entitled to put upon himself."[4]

Bear in mind the "direction" in which my argument moves. I start with features of the value that people ascribe to human life at whatever stage of development they think that it is morally murder to kill a human being. Though people on opposing sides of the abortion dispute differ on when this stage is reached, they agree that, once it is reached, the life of particular living human beings has asymmetric value compared to the life of future possible human beings. I use this fact as a keyhole from which we can trace the shape of the sought-after key to the abortion problem. I look for some property that characterizes human beings (at some point) and that can reasonably be valued asymmetrically. I identify this property as people's subjective valuation of their lives, and I characterize the valuing of this property as respect. But note that my argument does not hinge on proving that we should respect people's subjective valuation of their lives. Rather, my main claim is that *only* our respect for people's subjective valuation of their lives can account for the way in which we normally think murder is immoral. Since such an account will only succeed if it shows our thinking about the immorality of murder to be reasonable, I try to

---

4. Immanuel Kant, "The Metaphysical Principles of Virtue," pt. 2 of *The Metaphysics of Morals*, in *Ethical Philosophy*, trans. James W. Ellington (Indianapolis, IN: Hackett, 1983; originally published 1797), 114.

show that we have good reason to respect people's subjective valuation of their lives.[5]

Since fetuses are not conscious that they are alive, they do not possess the property that is the object of asymmetric valuing, and thus there is no ground for according them the special protection to which we think human life (at some point) is entitled. Neither, of course, are infants conscious that they are alive. I claim in that case that the indirect valuing of respect is also at work; however, the respect is aimed, not at the infants, but at the people who love them. People generally (not just parents or relatives) do (and I contend that it is good that they do) love infants—a love I link to the sentiment that Hume called "humanity" and that he understood as a general affection for our conspecifics. Respect for this love gives us a strong reason not to kill infants. I think that a similar ground will provide a strong reason not to kill severely retarded individuals or victims of senile dementia.

Moreover, I shall argue that, as humans develop into children and then adults, they are rightly granted autonomy rights which further imply the wrongness of killing them. Indeed, my argument about abortion is set within a larger analysis of the ways in which our valuation and protection of human life changes in appropriate response to changes in the development of humans themselves, so that the lives of infants, of young children, of older children and adults, and of severely

---

5. Some readers will have noted that the notion of asymmetric value is close to what moral philosophers call the *inviolability of persons*, according to which it is wrong to violate people's rights even as a means to produce a net reduction of such violations generally. This has posed a problem for recent moral theorists, since it seems that, if such violations are bad, then it is better to produce fewer than to allow more. What inviolability shares with asymmetry is a rejection of the moral fungibility of human beings. Asymmetry rejects the moral fungibility of human beings by denying that evil done to existing human beings can be canceled out by good done to (or derived from) future possible ones, whereas inviolability rejects fungibility by denying that evil done to existing human beings can be canceled out by good done to other existing ones. Inviolability is a stronger restriction than asymmetry, because existing humans have stronger claims on us than possible ones; but inviolability presupposes asymmetry. One could hardly believe that the fates of existing human beings are not fungible with each other while believing that the fates of existing humans are fungible with the fates of future possible humans. Consequently, if my solution to the problem of asymmetry is correct, it will be part of the solution to the problem of inviolability. For a sampling of comments on inviolability, see Robert Nozick, *Anarchy, State, and Utopia* (New York: Basic Books, 1974), 30; Samuel Scheffler, *The Rejection of Consequentialism* (Oxford: Oxford University Press, 1982), 88–89; F. M. Kamm, "Non-consequentialism, the Person as an End-in-Itself, and the Significance of Status," *Philosophy and Public Affairs* 21, no. 4 (Fall 1992): 383; Thomas Nagel, *Equality and Partiality* (New York: Oxford University Press, 1991), 148–49.

retarded or demented humans are appropriately valued—and appropriately protected—in different ways. In fact, this argument can be extended before birth and after death to account for the special treatment to be accorded to aborted fetuses and human corpses. All of this will be developed further in chapter 3, where possible objections will also be considered.

Basic Terms

Abortion

By "abortion," I mean the intentional termination of pregnancy either by killing the fetus directly or by removing the fetus from the womb with the result that it dies. Surgical removal of a viable fetus that lives on is, then, not abortion. It terminates pregnancy, but it does not result in the death of the fetus.

Fetus or *Embryo*

For simplicity's sake, I follow the widespread, though technically incorrect, practice of using the term *fetus* (and sometimes *embryo*) to refer to the being that develops in a pregnant woman from the moment of conception to the moment of birth. The scientific terminology is stricter than this: The single cell that results from the fertilization of the egg is a *zygote*. Shortly thereafter, when it becomes somewhat more complex, it is a *blastocyst*. When it implants in the uterine wall about six days after fertilization, it is a called an *embryo*. It is technically a *fetus* only at about sixty days after conception.[6]

Some people think that using the term *fetus* or *embryo* prejudices the discussion by dehumanizing the occupant of the pregnant woman's uterus. The alternative would be to use the term *baby*, but this surely prejudices the discussion in the other direction. I shall stick closer to the scientific terminology by using *fetus* or *embryo*, and hope that readers—now alerted to the possible prejudicial effects of the terminology—will not be swayed one way or the other by the language. A similar problem arises regarding pronouns. Shall we speak of the fetus as *it*, or as *him or her*? I shall use *it* and, here too, rely on alerted readers not to read anything pro or con into this usage.

6. See Harold J. Morowitz and James S. Trefil, *The Facts of Life* (New York: Oxford University Press, 1992), 46.

Pro-life and Pro-choice

I refer to the position that takes abortion to be morally murder as *pro-life*, and the position that takes abortion to be morally permissible as *pro-choice*. But *pro-life* and *pro-choice* are political labels, not technically accurate philosophical terms. I use them because of their familiarity, not because I think that only pro-lifers are pro-life or that only pro-choicers are pro-choice.

Right to Life and Moral Vulnerability to Murder

Though I shall speak of other writers who claim or deny that the fetus has a right to life, I do not think that the question of abortion should be posed as whether the fetus has a right to life. Exclusive focus on the right to life is unsatisfactory for two reasons. First, there could be ways in which it is wrong to kill fetuses other than because they possess a right to life. We could have a *duty* not to kill some beings even though those beings have no right to life. The Ten Commandments' prohibition on killing makes no reference to, or presumption of, rights. It establishes a duty not to kill human beings based on God's will, not on those human beings' right to life. Also, we seem to have a duty not to be cruel to animals though it would be odd to think that animals have a right to noncruel treatment. Consequently, we might have a duty not to take fetuses' lives even though they do not have a right to life. We should not narrow the range of possible solutions to the abortion problem in advance by assuming that the only way in which it is morally wrong to be responsible for a being's death is that the being has a right not to be killed.[7]

The second reason that the exclusive focus on a right to life is too narrow is this. A right to life is normally understood as a right not to be killed and thus as a *negative* requirement that we refrain from taking life. But it is also possible that fetuses have rights to *positive* assistance or protection. After all, it seems that small children have rights to positive assistance from adults (and not just from their parents) to protect, feed, and educate them. Particularly vulnerable humans generally, and fetuses in particular, might have *positive* rights to our assistance to protect them against threats to their lives or well-being.

---

7. This mistake is all too prevalent in the literature on the abortion question, although, in a recent article, James Q. Wilson makes the mistake in reverse. He distinguishes the rights-based approach to abortion from the moral approach. Apparently, he has never heard of moral rights. I shall try to steer clear of both errors. See James Q. Wilson, "On Abortion," *Commentary* 27, no. 1 (January 1994): 21–29.

The upshot of this is that focusing exclusively on whether a fetus has a right to life (conventionally understood) ignores at least two other ways in which it might be immoral to abort a fetus: Either we might have a duty not to kill it or the fetus might have a positive right to our protection. To cast our net as widely as possible, then, we should ask, not simply whether a fetus has a right to life, but rather whether it has *any moral status that would make it gravely morally wrong to kill it or to cause it to die.*

I call that moral status *vulnerability to murder*, though *murder* is always meant strictly as a moral term, not as a legal one. A being is *vulnerable to murder* if, all things being equal, intentionally killing it or causing it to die would be roughly as morally wrong as killing a human child or adult (in the absence of excusing conditions, such as self-defense and so on). Now, the immorality of killing human children or adults is asymmetric, that is, much worse than not procreating. So if a being is vulnerable to murder, it has a moral right to asymmetric protection of its life, that is, to protection against being killed and replaced. Consequently, if we find that there is no plausible ground for valuing fetuses asymmetrically, that will imply that there is no plausible ground for holding it gravely immoral to kill or cause the death of fetuses in the way that we hold it gravely immoral to kill children or adults—and thus that abortion is not, morally speaking, murder.

Humans and *Persons*

Though some pro-choicers question whether the fetus is a human being, I think this is a confusion. There can be no doubt, in my view, that the fetus is a human organism. And many who have argued for the moral permissibility of abortion have granted this fact. For example, Laura Purdy and Michael Tooley write, "A fetus developing inside a human mother is certainly an organism belonging to *Homo sapiens* [the human species]."[8] And Mary Anne Warren does not doubt that the fetus is human in "the *genetic* sense," that is, "the sense in which *any* member of the species is a human being."[9] All of these writers distinguish this genetic or *biological* sense of human from the *moral*

---

8. Laura Purdy and Michael Tooley, "Is Abortion Murder?" in *Abortion, Pro and Con*, ed. Robert Perkins (Cambridge, MA: Schenckman, 1974), 140.

9. Mary Anne Warren, "On the Moral and Legal Status of Abortion," in *The Problem of Abortion*, ed. Joel Feinberg, 2nd ed. (Belmont, CA: Wadsworth, 1984), 110 (emphasis in original). See also Morowitz and Trefil, who think abortion is permissible until the end of the second trimester of pregnancy but accept that the fetus is a human organism from conception on. Morowitz and Trefil, *The Facts of Life*, 16.

sense according to which being human entitles one to certain moral rights, including normally the right to life. These writers use the term *person* to signify human in the moral sense—where a *person* is a bearer of moral rights including a right to life.

I follow this usage and mean by *human* the biological or genetic sense in which anything that is the offspring of human parents, that possesses a human genetic code and so on, is human. I shall use the term *person* to mean a human in the moral sense, that is, one who possesses moral rights and the moral status of vulnerability to murder. The question of abortion, then, is whether the human fetus is a person.

Note that, in this question, the term *person* is being used *formally*, rather than *substantively*. Substantively, a person is a certain kind of being, say, one who possesses reason or self-consciousness. Formally, a person is simply a "bearer of moral rights." This is formal, or we might say *merely* formal, since it does not specify what kind of being something must be to be a bearer of moral rights. Normally, the context will suffice to make clear which sense of *person* I am using. However, when there is any chance of misunderstanding, I will add the adjective *formal* or *substantive* to *person* to indicate which sense is meant.

Many philosophers assume that being a substantive person qualifies one for the rights that go with formal personhood. This is certainly the conventional practice. Nonetheless, if we are to understand why human beings are entitled to formal personhood, we will need an account of why the traits associated with substantial personhood are appropriate grounds for the attribution of asymmetric value. In the course of my argument, I shall present such an account.

Overview

This book is divided into three chapters. The first reviews the history of attitudes and laws about abortion in the West. The second reviews the main arguments about the morality of abortion—both pro-life and pro-choice—and shows that they fail. The third presents my own argument for the moral permissibility of abortion, as well as a sketch of the various ways in which we value human life from conception to death.

It may seem odd to begin an essay in moral philosophy with a chapter on history. There are two reasons for starting this way. First of all, this history will show that, in the West, the view that abortion is morally or legally equivalent to murder *from conception on*—that is, from the moment that the fetus begins to exist—has been the exception rather than the rule. In chapter 3, I shall claim that the wrongness of killing fetuses (or of killing human beings at any stage) hinges on their coming to possess some appropriate property (or properties), *not simply on their existing*. My review of the history shows at least that this idea has a long pedigree.

Second, this history is aimed at shedding light on the events leading up to the Supreme Court's crucial 1973 decision, *Roe v. Wade*, which effectively made abortion legal in the United States. I shall present key passages from the Court's decision as well as from the dissents. My purpose here is to bring out that, though *Roe v. Wade* has settled the constitutional status of abortion for the present, it is a solution to the *legal* problem, not a solution to the *moral* problem of abortion. As a legal solution, it is, I shall suggest, stronger than its critics contend. However, as is often the case with legal solutions to difficult social problems, it is a compromise between competing considerations—in particular, between a woman's right to control her body and the state's right to protect potential human life—and it is not a stable compromise. I shall argue that the only route to a stable resolution of the legal problem lies in a satisfactory solution to the moral problem—which the Court has tried to avoid, and which I shall try to provide.

In chapter 2, I consider the main arguments, pro and con, about the morality of abortion. I start with a number of arguments that attempt to settle the issue of its morality without addressing the question of the moral status of the fetus. While these approaches show that there are numerous moral issues apart from the question of the fetus's moral status, I shall argue that no solution to the moral problem is possible without settling that question. I pass then to arguments that focus on determining the moral status of the fetus. These arguments fail for a variety of reasons. Some assume that all members of the human species are vulnerable to murder, and thus fail to say what it is about humans that entitles them to this moral status. These arguments are forms of *speciesism*—a dogmatic preference for beings like us, which is as arbitrary and questionable as its analogues, *racism* and *sexism*. Some arguments appeal to the fact that a fetus is a *potential person*, that it will become a bearer of rights in the normal course of things—but this implies only that it will become a being that is vulnerable to murder, not that it is one now. Other arguments appeal to some trait of fetuses—such as sentience, the ability to experience pleasure and pain—that cannot plausibly ground a right to life because this appeal would imply that beings not normally thought to have a right to life—in the case of sentience, most animals—have the same right as human beings. Other arguments fail for yet other reasons, or combinations of reasons. But the most important and revealing ground of the failure of many of these arguments is that they cannot account for the asymmetric value that we attribute to human life when we think that it is gravely immoral to kill human beings.

In chapter 3, I shall use this asymmetric value as a clue to finding a solution to the moral problem of abortion. I shall argue that *only a certain kind of valuing of a being's own conscious valuing of its own life* can account for the asymmetric value that we place on human life when we think that it is gravely immoral to kill human beings. This shows that the point of our practice of morally condemning murder is aimed, not at preserving human life, but human *lives*, and not all human lives, but only human lives already underway and consciously so. If this is correct, it will follow that pro-lifers must give up the claim that abortion is murder. In this chapter, I address the problem of infanticide, I sketch a general theory of the ways we value human life, and I show that my solution to the problem of abortion complies with the terms appropriate to discourse in a liberal society.

1

Abortion, from Hammurabi's Code to *Roe v. Wade*

It is perhaps not generally appreciated that the restrictive criminal abortion laws in effect in a majority of States today [1973] are of relatively recent vintage. Those laws, generally proscribing abortion or its attempt at any time during pregnancy except when necessary to preserve the pregnant woman's life, are not of ancient or even common-law origin. Instead, they derive from statutory changes effected, for the most part, in the latter half of the 19th century.

Roe v. Wade (Justice Harry A. Blackmun, for the Court)

[W]hen couples have children in excess, let abortion be procured before sense and life have begun; what may or may not be lawfully done in these cases depends on the question of life and sensation.

Aristotle, *Politics*

If a person's right to life is violated at the moment in which he is first conceived in his mother's womb, an indirect blow is struck also at the whole of the moral order.

Pope John Paul II, homily at the Capitol Mall in Washington, D.C.

[T]he unborn have never been recognized in the law as persons in the whole sense.

Roe v. Wade (Justice Harry A. Blackmun, for the Court)

From Hammurabi's Code . . .

The earliest laws of relevance to abortion were not concerned with the voluntary termination of pregnancy by the pregnant woman. They were rules providing compensation for the death of a fetus resulting

15

from an assault on a pregnant woman.[1] Their goal appears to have been, not to protect the rights of fetuses, but to protect the rights of fathers. Articles 209 and 210 of The Code of Hammurabi (thought to have been written in the eighteenth century B.C.E.) provide: "If a seignior struck a[nother] seignior's daughter and has caused her to have a miscarriage, he shall pay ten shekels of silver for her fetus. If that woman has died, they shall put his daughter to death."[2] And a very famous passage of the Hebrew Torah, or Old Testament (Exodus 21:22–25), reads: "If, when men come to blows, they hurt a woman who is pregnant and she suffers a miscarriage, though she does not die of it, the man responsible must pay the compensation demanded of him by the woman's master; he shall hand it over after arbitration. But should she die, you shall give life for life, eye for eye, tooth for tooth, hand for hand, foot for foot, burn for burn, wound for wound, stroke for stroke." Traditionally, this has been interpreted as showing that the fetus did not have the same status as the pregnant woman in Hebrew law.[3] But abortion as such—voluntarily induced termination of pregnancy—is not mentioned in the Hebrew Bible.[4]

Some five centuries after Hammurabi's code, the Middle Assyrian laws appear to be the first to penalize voluntary abortion, providing gruesome punishment—impalement and no burial—for a woman who "has a miscarriage by her own act."[5] Interestingly, this was in a society in which fathers had the right to practice infanticide on their unwanted offspring. Clearly, then, this law was not meant to protect fetuses. It appears rather to have been aimed at keeping the decision about which offspring live or die in the hands of their fathers.[6]

---

1. Jean Gray Platt et al., eds., "Special Project: Survey of Abortion Law," *Arizona State Law Journal* 67 (1980): 74–76.

2. Quoted in Platt et al., eds., "Survey of Abortion Law," 74 n. 5. Note that, instead of the Christian expressions B.C. and A.D. ("before Christ" and *anno Domini*, or "year of the Lord"), I use the more neutral expressions B.C.E. and C.E. ("before the common era" and "common era").

3. John Connery, S. J., *Abortion: The Development of the Roman Catholic Perspective* (Chicago: Loyola University Press, 1977), 11. The *Torah* (sometimes translated as "the Law") is comprised of the Hebrew Five Books of Moses (also called the Pentateuch). The Hebrew Bible consists of the Torah as well as the *Neviim* (the Prophets), and the *Ketuvim* (or Holy Writings), which includes Psalms and Chronicles and other writings. The Hebrew Bible is also called the *Old Testament*, though this terminology is distinctively Christian in suggesting that the Hebrew Bible is the precursor of the *New Testament*, whose religious validity is not accepted by Jews.

4. Kristin Luker, *Abortion and the Politics of Motherhood* (Berkeley, CA: University of California Press, 1984), 12.

5. Platt et al., eds., "Survey of Abortion Law," 75 and n. 7.

6. See Gerda Lerner, *The Creation of Patriarchy* (New York: Oxford University Press, 1986), 120–21.

The ancient Greek philosophers were generally tolerant of abortion. In his *Republic,* Plato (c. 427–347 B.C.E.) recommended aborting offspring of undesirable unions.[7] And Aristotle (384–322 B.C.E.) thought abortion was a proper means to limit family size.[8] Among ancient Greek schools of thought, only the Pythagoreans were categorically opposed to all abortions, holding that the soul entered the body at conception and that abortion was equivalent to murder. The Pythagoreans, rather than Hippocrates himself, are believed to have been responsible for the passage in the Hippocratic Oath that prohibits assisting a woman to bring about an abortion: "I will give no deadly medicine to anyone if asked, nor suggest any such counsel; and in like manner I will not give a woman a remedy to produce abortion."[9] The doubt about whether Hippocrates actually wrote the prohibition on abortion in the oath attributed to him is due to the fact that Hippocrates (c. 460–377 B.C.E.) believed that fetuses became animated, not at conception, but on the thirtieth day of gestation for male fetuses and the forty-second day for females.[10]

We see here with Hippocrates an idea that would get its classical formulation a century later in the writings of Aristotle, namely, that the fetus does not develop or receive a human soul until some time after conception. Since the Latin word for "soul" is *anima,* this theory came to be called the theory of *delayed animation.* The soul is, for Aristotle, "the cause of the living body as the original source of local movement."[11] He thought that "[i]n the case of male children the first movement usually occurs on . . . about the fortieth day [of gestation], but if the child be a female then on . . . about the ninetieth day,"[12] and Aristotle took this as evidence that the soul was present in male fetuses at the fortieth day and in female fetuses at the ninetieth.[13] In Aristotle's

---

7. Plato, *Republic,* 5.461c, trans. Paul Shorey, in *Plato: The Collected Dialogues,* ed. Edith Hamilton and Huntington Cairns (Princeton, NJ: Princeton University Press, 1989), 700.

8. Aristotle, *Politics,* 7.16.1335b, in *The Complete Works of Aristotle,* ed. Jonathan Barnes (Princeton, NJ: Princeton University Press, 1984), vol. 2, p. 2119.

9. Platt et al., eds., "Survey of Abortion Law," 78. Cf. *Roe v. Wade,* 410 U.S. at 131, for variations in wording of the Hippocratic Oath. I have combined several formulations to arrive at one most easily understood.

10. Platt et al., eds., "Survey of Abortion Law," 78; Glanville Williams, *The Sanctity of Life and the Criminal Law* (London: Faber & Faber, 1958), 149.

11. Aristotle, *On the Soul,* 2.4.415b, in *Complete Works,* ed. Barnes, vol. 1, p. 661.

12. Aristotle, *History of Animals,* 7.3.583b, in *Complete Works,* ed. Barnes, vol. 1, p. 914.

13. See, for example, *The HarperCollins Encyclopedia of Catholicism,* ed. Richard P. McBrien (New York: HarperCollins, 1995), 4.

view, of equal importance with movement as an indicator of the presence of the soul is the fetus's taking on of human form, for Aristotle thought that all things are made of matter and form and that the form of a human being is its soul. So, for example, Aristotle commented that asking "whether the soul and body are one" is like asking "whether the wax and its shape are one."[14] At the same time that the fetus first moves, he thought, it also "begins to resolve into distinct parts, it having hitherto consisted of a fleshlike substance without distinction of parts."[15] As a result of Aristotle's enormous influence, during antiquity and the middle ages, *formation* and *movement*—which came to be called in English law, *quickening*[16]—were taken as indicators of the *animation*, or *ensoulment*, of the fetus. Thus, it was widely believed that the fetus received a human soul some substantial period of time after conception.

Interestingly, in the Septuagint (the Greek translation of the Torah produced in Alexandria in the third century B.C.E.), which was influenced by Greek and especially Aristotelian philosophy, we find a quite different rendering of Exodus 21:22–25 from the Hebrew one we saw at the beginning of this chapter. The Greek version distinguishes the penalty for causing a woman to miscarry an *unformed* fetus from that for causing miscarriage of a *formed* fetus. In the case of an unformed fetus, the penalty is a fine, whereas for a formed one, the penalty is death.[17] This distinction was applied to Christian legal and theological arguments by the early church father Tertullian (c. 160–c. 230 C.E.) in his *De Anima*.[18]

Indeed, throughout the period from ancient Greece to the nineteenth century, we find references to animated, formed, or quickened fetuses to signify fetuses that have been ensouled at some point after conception. Note, however, that different thinkers took the relations between these various notions differently. For example, there are some who took formation as identical to ensoulment and others who took it as the precondition of ensoulment. Likewise with the other concepts.

---

14. Aristotle, *On the Soul*, 2.1.412b, in *Complete Works*, ed. Barnes, vol. 1, p. 657.

15. Aristotle, *History of Animals*, 7.3.583b, in *Complete Works*, ed. Barnes, vol. 1, p. 914. This is not to imply that the fetus has no form at all prior to receiving a human soul. Aristotle held that matter never exists without form. Prior to receiving the rational soul that would make it human, the fetus has the form that comes with a nutritive (vegetative) soul and an animal soul.

16. Connery, *Roman Catholic Perspective*, 213, inter alia.

17. Connery, *Roman Catholic Perspective*, 17; see also *The HarperCollins Encyclopedia of Catholicism*, 4. In the Septuagint version, no mention is made of injury to the pregnant woman.

18. Luker, *Abortion and the Politics of Motherhood*, 13 n.

Nothing in the discussion that follows, however, hinges on the details of the various relations between *formation, animation, quickening,* and *ensoulment.* What is crucial is that all of these terms signify a point *after* conception—normally from six to sixteen weeks after conception—at which the fetus is in some important sense finally thought to be enough like a human child or adult to make killing it uniquely grave, more like murder than like contraception.

The Stoics went much further than Aristotle, holding that a fetus becomes a living human being at birth when it takes its first breath (*anima* means "breath" as well as "soul").[19] Due to the influence of Stoicism, the Romans placed no restrictions on abortion. They regarded the fetus as *pars viscerum matris,* "part of the mother's internal organs."[20] "Roman law explicitly held that the 'child in the belly of its mother' was not a person, and hence abortion was not murder. . . . [S]uch legal regulation of abortion as existed in the Roman Empire was designed primarily to protect the rights of fathers rather than the rights of embryos."[21] Infanticide was declared to be homicide after Rome adopted Christianity as its official religion, but legal tolerance of abortion continued even in Christian times.[22]

During the same period, the Jewish Mishnah proclaimed a moderate view of abortion. The Mishnah is a digest of the oral tradition of the Hebrew laws (the Oral Torah) that was compiled around 200 C.E. The rabbinic commentaries on the Mishnah are known as the Talmud. The Mishnah expressly allows for killing the fetus to save the life of the pregnant woman. However, once most of the offspring's body has come out of the womb, killing it would be murder, and murdering one human being to save another is forbidden. Thus, while in Jewish teaching abortion at any stage is a serious offense, the rabbis effectively treated only born babies as morally comparable to human children or adults.[23]

Though the New Testament (like the Hebrew Bible) is silent on abortion, early Christians opposed abortion at any point during pregnancy,

---

19. Williams, *Sanctity of Life,* 149, cited in Platt et al., eds., "Survey of Abortion Law," 77–78. Note the relation between the words *spirit* and *respiration* in English.

20. Lawrence Lader, *Abortion* (Boston, MA: Beacon Press, 1966), 76; cited in Platt et al., eds., "Survey of Abortion Law," 80.

21. Luker, *Abortion and the Politics of Motherhood,* 12.

22. John T. Noonan, Jr., *Contraception: A History of Its Treatment by the Catholic Theologians and Canonists,* enlarged ed. (Cambridge: Harvard University Press, 1986), 86.

23. Louis Jacobs, *The Jewish Religion: A Companion* (New York: Oxford University Press, 1995), pp. 11–12, 349–50, 369; Connery, *Roman Catholic Perspective,* 11, 15.

even if they distinguished between the aborting of formed and unformed fetuses. There was a general condemnation of abortion in the
Didache (also known as *The Teaching of the Twelve Apostles*), which
stemmed from the Jewish community but eventually became a docu-
ment of early Christianity. Other early church documents, such as the
Epistle of the Pseudo-Barnabas and Athenagoras's *Plea for Christians*, con-
demn all abortion as homicide.[24] The Council of Elvira in Spain in 305
and the Council of Ancyra in Galatia in 314 both condemned abortion,
the former prescribing permanent excommunication, the latter allowing for penance and eventual reconciliation with the sinner.[25] The
wholesale prohibition on abortion was moderated somewhat under
the influence of the great theologians Saints Augustine (354–430) and
Jerome (c. 340–420). Augustine distinguished abortion of an *embryo in-
formatus* (a fetus prior to ensoulment) from that of an *embryo formatus*
(an ensouled fetus). He maintained that the first should be punished
by a fine and the second by death. Jerome thought that abortion is not
murder until the fetus has developed into recognizably human form,
but nonetheless regarded abortion at any point (and contraception as
well) as a grave sin.[26]

A greater acceptance of abortion began to characterize European society in the twelfth century. Medical schools began to teach physicians
how to induce abortion by means of drugs or violent movements. Avi-
cenna's *Canon of Medicine* asserted that abortion could be resorted to if
it was necessary to save the pregnant woman's life. Recipes for abortifacient potions were commonly included in digests of European folk
medicine. When the monk John Gratian (died c. 1160) codified the
canon law in approximately 1140, he followed Augustine in holding
that the soul does not enter the fetus until the fetus is formed, and he

---

24. Connery, *Roman Catholic Perspective*, 35–37; see also *The HarperCollins Encyclopedia of Catholicism*, 5.

25. Connery, *Roman Catholic Perspective*, 46–47. Luker claims that these penalties were directed only at those women who procured an abortion after com-
mitting a sexual crime such as adultery or prostitution. See Luker, *Abortion and
the Politics of Motherhood*, 12.

26. Platt et al., eds., "Survey of Abortion Law," 84. "Latin Church Fathers
Jerome (d. 420) and Augustine (d. 430) both taught that abortion is not homicide until the 'scattered elements' are formed into a body" (*The HarperCollins
Encyclopedia of Catholicism*, 5). See also Noonan, *Contraception*, 88, 90, 136. Early
Christians regarded contraception as a sin because they regarded sexuality
negatively (as the means by which original sin was transmitted) and believed
its only justification was procreation. Moreover, contraception violated "the
order of nature, which called for the depositing of the male semen in the vas
of the female." See *The HarperCollins Encyclopedia of Catholicism*, 178–81 (quotation from p. 179).

concluded that abortion prior to ensoulment is not murder. At the time, the church held to a variation of the Aristotelian theory, according to which male fetuses are endowed with a soul on the fortieth day of gestation and female fetuses on the eightieth. Most significantly, the church began to view abortion prior to ensoulment as a much less serious sin than it had in the centuries since Augustine and Jerome.[27] Peter Lombard (1095–1160), like Gratian, followed Augustine and Jerome in holding that abortion is not homicide unless the fetus is formed and ensouled. Innocent III, who was pope from 1198 to 1216, held that killing a fetus is homicide only if the fetus is formed or animated. And Albert the Great, who was the teacher of Aquinas, agreed with Peter Lombard.[28]

The Aristotelian doctrine (called *hylomorphism*) that all things are composed of matter and form was embraced by Saint Thomas Aquinas in the thirteenth century, and adopted officially by the Roman Catholic Church at the Council of Vienne in 1312.[29] Aquinas largely accepted the Aristotelian account of gestation, including the different rates of development of male and female fetuses. He, too, insisted that it is the killing of an animated fetus that counts as homicide.[30] Replying to an objection, Aquinas wrote: "He that strikes a woman with child does something unlawful: wherefore if there results the death either of the woman or of the animated fetus, he will not be excused from homicide.[31] Aquinas also placed great emphasis on the soul as the source of movement of the living human body, and this may have contributed to the increasing focus on movement—quickening—as marking the point at which the fetus is ensouled: "The soul does not move the body by its essence, as the form of the body, but by the motive power, the act of which presupposes the body to be already actualized by the soul."[32]

Henry de Bracton (died 1268) was the first writer of a secular legal treatise to mention abortion. Though almost all abortion cases were

---

27. Platt et al., eds., "Survey of Abortion Law," 86–87; Connery, *Roman Catholic Perspective*, 58, 90.

28. Connery, *Roman Catholic Perspective*, 96–97, 106–107; see also Noonan, *Contraception*, 211, 232.

29. Joseph F. Donceel, S. J., "A Liberal Catholic View," in *The Problem of Abortion*, ed. Joel Feinberg, 2nd ed. (Belmont, CA: Wadsworth, 1984), 16.

30. Connery, *Roman Catholic Perspective*, 110–12.

31. St. Thomas Aquinas, *Summa Theologica*, pt. 2–2, Q. 64, art. 8, reply to obj. 2 (Westminster, MD: Christian Classics, 1948), vol. 3, p. 1466.

32. Aquinas, *Summa Theologica*, pt. 1, Q. 76, art. 4, reply to obj. 2; vol. 1, p. 377; see also Aquinas, *Summa Contra Gentiles*, trans. James F. Anderson (Notre Dame, IN: University of Notre Dame Press, 1975), bk. 2, chaps. 88–89, pp. 296–308.

handled in English ecclesiastical courts, in his *Laws and Customs of England*, Bracton asserted that English common law viewed abortion as homicide only if it occurred after the fetus was "formed or animated."[33] As to when the fetus was "formed or animated," the crucial point was the quickening.[34]

By the close of the thirteenth century, the quickening doctrine was firmly established in English common law. This made for a remarkably tolerant standard. Quickening, or fetal movement, normally occurs between the sixteenth and eighteenth weeks of pregnancy—well after either the fortieth or the eightieth day, and likewise well after the fetus takes on recognizable human form. Moreover, courts interpreted the quickening as occurring when the pregnant woman first *felt* movement in her womb. Consequently, the only witness to its occurrence was the pregnant woman herself or possibly her husband, neither of whom was likely to testify to it if the woman was accused of the crime of abortion.[35]

Subsequent developments served to weaken the standard further. In 1644, in his posthumously published *Institutes of the Laws of England*, Sir Edward Coke (1552–1634) held that abortion prior to quickening was not a common-law crime at all and that abortion after quickening was only a misdemeanor. The latter became a felony (murder) only if the offspring was born alive and died afterwards as a result of the abortion.[36] A century later, Sir William Blackstone (1723–1780) followed Coke. In his *Commentaries on the Laws of England*, published in 1765, Blackstone pointed out that where a pregnant woman convicted of a capital offense "plead[ed] her pregnancy," the judge would ask "a jury of twelve matrons or discreet women" to determine the state of the pregnancy. "[I]f they [brought] in their verdict *quick with child* (for barely, *with child*, unless it be alive in the womb, [was] not sufficient)," her execution would be delayed until she gave birth.[37] According to

---

33. Platt et al., eds., "Survey of Abortion Law," 87; Noonan, *Contraception*, 216. There is some doubt now about whether Bracton is really the author of *De legibus et consuetudinibus Angliae (The laws and customs of England)*. See J. H. Burns, ed., *The Cambridge History of Medieval Political Thought, c. 350–c. 1450* (Cambridge: Cambridge University Press, 1988), 663.
34. Connery, *Roman Catholic Perspective*, 213, inter alia.
35. Platt et al., eds., "Survey of Abortion Law," 88.
36. Edward Coke, *Institutes of the Laws of England* (Buffalo, NY: W. S. Hein, 1986; originally published 1644), vol. 3, p. 50; cited in Platt et al., eds., "Survey of Abortion Law," 89.
37. William Blackstone, *Commentaries on the Laws of England*, 21st ed. (London: Sweet, Maxwell, Stevens & Norton, 1844; originally published 1765), vol. 4, pp. 394–95 (emphasis in original).

Blackstone, "Life . . . begins in contemplation of law as soon as an infant is able to stir in the mother's womb."[38]

This tolerant common-law standard was still in effect in nineteenth century America when state legislatures began to pass the very strict anti-abortion laws that the Supreme Court later overturned in *Roe v. Wade.* Indeed, as James Mohr writes, "American courts pointedly sustained the most lenient implications of the quickening doctrine even after the British themselves had abandoned them."[39]

I shall return to this point shortly. For the moment, note as well that the Catholic position was still undergoing change. In 1591, Pope Gregory XIV restricted the penalty of excommunication to only those responsible for aborting an animated fetus. Starting in the seventeenth century, however, increasing medical knowledge about reproduction and embryology led to growing doubts about the doctrine of delayed animation. Fetal growth appeared more and more a continuous matter, with no significant breaks between conception and birth. In 1853, Ferdinand Kember discovered that conception is produced by the male sperm entering the female ovum. Since, in Aristotelian doctrine, the male sperm carries the soul, this discovery implied that ensoulment takes place at conception. Increasingly, the Roman Catholic Church insisted that abortion is gravely wrong at any point after conception. In 1869, Pope Pius IX removed the distinction between animated and unanimated fetuses from the canon law, thus providing excommunication for causing abortion at any stage of fetal development.[40]

In the new American nation, because the lenient common-law standard prevailed, the situation at the beginning of the 19th century was quite tolerant regarding abortion. "Consequently," writes Luker, "in nineteenth-century America, as in medieval Europe, first trimester abortions, and a goodly number of second trimester abortions as well, faced little legal regulation."[41] Numerous home medical manuals—

---

38. "Life is the immediate gift of God, a right inherent by nature in every individual; and it begins in contemplation of law as soon as an infant is able to stir in the mother's womb. For if a woman is quick with child, and by a potion or otherwise, killeth it in her womb; or, if any one beat her, whereby the child dieth in her body, and she is delivered of a dead child; this, though not murder, was by the ancient law homicide and manslaughter. But the modern law doth not look upon this offence in quite so atrocious a light, but merely as a heinous misdemesnor [*sic*]" (Blackstone, *Commentaries on the Laws of England*, vol. 1, p. 129).

39. James C. Mohr, *Abortion in America: The Origins and Evolution of National Policy, 1800–1900* (New York: Oxford University Press, 1978), 5.

40. See Mohr, *Abortion in America*, 36–37; Lader, *Abortion*, 80–81; Connery, *Roman Catholic Perspective*, 168–70, 187, 208–9, 211–12; Noonan, *Contraception*, 405.

41. Luker, *Abortion and the Politics of Motherhood*, 14.

frequently written expressly for women—contained information about how to induce abortion, often in the form of advice on how to remove blockages to normal menstrual flow. Among these were William Buchan's *Domestic Medicine* (probably the most widely consulted one; continually reprinted from 1782 through 1850), Samuel K. Jennings's *Married Lady's Companion* (which "had its second printing in 1808 and was intended for women in rural areas"), Joseph Brevitt's *Female Medical Repository* (1810), and Thomas Ewell's *Letter to Ladies* (1817). Ewell was "a surgeon at Navy Hospital in Washington, D.C. . . . , who wrote forthrightly about unblocking obstructed menses." Like the other books just mentioned, Ewell's

> urged hot sitz baths, doses of aloes, and a number of straining exercises. Walking, horseback riding, and jumping, the more the better, all helped bring on abortion, he counseled, especially at the time menses would normally have occurred had the last period not been missed. Ewell [also] thought electricity through the thighs might end a suppression [of menstrual flow] and that light bleeding could be beneficial. To those rather elemental staples, Ewell added some medically more advanced ideas including internal douching with strong brandy, water as hot as could be tolerated, vinegar, wine, or strong brine.[42]

In addition to early-nineteenth-century home medical manuals, Americans seeking information about abortifacients, as well as abortions themselves, could consult midwives and herbal healers ("so-called Indian doctors"). Mohr speculates that, because of the impossibility of confidently diagnosing pregnancy in its early stages and because of the common acceptance of procedures to treat for amenorrhea (blocked menses), many regular (formally trained or apprenticed) physicians performed early abortions. And, says Mohr, "this practice was neither morally nor legally wrong in the eyes of the vast majority of Americans, provided it was accomplished before quickening."[43] Leslie Reagan maintains that both the willingness of physicians (in private) to perform early abortions and the popular view that these abortions

---

42. Mohr, *Abortion in America*, 6–10, 266 n. 6. Dr. Buchan, author of *Domestic Medicine*, was unusual in that, from 1797 on, he added to new editions of his book a forceful denunciation of abortion at any time during pregnancy. See Luker, *Abortion and the Politics of Motherhood*, 24.

43. Mohr, *Abortion in America*, 11, 14–16. "Contemporary observers . . . were in unanimous agreement that the women who engaged in abortion did not believe that they were doing anything wrong. The common law tradition, they argued, led women to feel that abortion was morally blameless, only slightly different from preventing a conception in the first place" (Luker, *Abortion and the Politics of Motherhood*, 20).

were morally acceptable continued throughout the period of legal repression that was to come.[44]

The first American statute concerning abortion was enacted by Connecticut in 1821. Prior to that date, there appears to have been no prosecution of abortion under the common law.[45] The Connecticut statute itself did little more than restate the common-law rule as interpreted by Blackstone, inasmuch as it provided punishment only for abortions performed after quickening. Over the next two decades, seven more states passed abortion laws similar to Connecticut's.

Things began to change in the 1840s. According to Mohr, "Medical writers throughout the period [agreed] unanimously . . . that the incidence of abortion rose dramatically around 1840." Moreover, abortion became more publicly visible. "During the 1840s, Americans . . . learned for the first time not only that many practitioners would provide abortion services, but that some practitioners had made the abortion business their chief livelihood. Indeed, abortion became one of the first specialties in American medical history[!]" In thinly veiled terms (referring to "Female complaints, such as Suppressions [of menses,]" and "private diseases"; promising "Good accommodations for ladies" and "Strict secrecy"), advertising for abortion services, by regular physicians and by irregulars, such as midwives, significantly increased. And there was more coverage by the popular press of "sensational trials alleged to involve botched abortions." The business of selling abortifacient medicines also boomed, as evidenced by the rising number of advertisements for such products as "Madame Restell's Female Pills, Drunette's Lunar Pills, Dr. Peter's French Renovating Pills . . . , Dr. Monroe's French Periodical Pills . . . , Dr. Melveau's Portuguese Female Pills," each said to produce miscarriage, though this advice was sometimes couched as a "warning" to pregnant women not to take the pills.[46]

Also starting in the 1840s, there was a change in the social character of abortion, or at least in the perception of its social character. Whereas,

---

44. Leslie J. Reagan, *When Abortion Was a Crime: Women, Medicine and Law in the United States, 1867–1973* (Berkeley, CA: University of California Press, 1997), 20. Marvin Olasky agrees that the regular medical profession in the nineteenth century was far from unanimous in its opposition to, or even unwillingness to perform, abortions. This continued into the early decades of the twentieth century, with physicians complaining about the willingness of many of their colleagues to perform abortions in spite of the official stand of the profession as represented by the AMA. Olasky also notes the general public tolerance of the practice at the time. Marvin Olasky, *Abortion Rites: A Social History of Abortion in America* (Washington, DC: Regnery, 1992), 123–25, 222–24, 227–33.

45. Platt et al., eds., "Survey of Abortion Law," 93.

46. Mohr, *Abortion in America*, 46–49, 53, 75, 79.

prior to this era, abortion had been seen as the recourse of unmarried women desperate to avoid the stigma of unwed motherhood, now it seemed that more married women were resorting to abortion to limit family size. This, at least, was the opinion widely held by regular physicians.[47] Regular physicians also believed that abortion was far more prevalent among Protestant women than among Catholics and, though numerous immigrant abortionists catered to other immigrants, more prevalent among native-born than among immigrant women. Similarly, the medical profession was sure that the practice was growing among middle- and upper-class women, and the relatively high prices of the procedure supply some support for this view. There is demographic evidence of a steep drop in the birthrate for native-born women (as distinct from immigrant women) after 1840, a drop large enough to lead to an overall decline in the birthrate throughout the nation compared to earlier in the century. However, the evidence that this was due to abortion is based largely on the opinions of regular physicians, who were, as we shall see, not disinterested observers.[48]

In 1840, Maine became the first state to clearly prohibit abortion at any stage of pregnancy. Its statute provided:

> Every person, who shall administer to any woman pregnant with child, *whether such child be quick or not*, any medicine, drug or substance whatever, or shall use or employ any instrument or other means whatever, with intent to destroy such child, and shall thereby destroy such child before its birth, *unless the same shall have been done as necessary to preserve the life of the mother*, shall be punished by imprisonment in the state prison, *not more than five years*, or by fine, not exceeding one thousand dollars, and imprisonment in the county jail, not more than one year.[49]

This statute was still in force when the U.S. Supreme Court issued its decision in *Roe v. Wade* 133 years later. Note that, though the statute treats abortion as a crime at any time after conception, it does not treat it as equivalent to murder. The penalties are much lighter than those normally provided for murder, and an exception is allowed for abor-

---

47. Mohr, *Abortion in America*, 86–90. Olasky maintains that "the evidence suggests that most abortions during that period [the middle decades of the nineteenth century] were related to prostitution." The evidence that Olasky presents are the judgments of contemporary commentators and the difficulty that prostitutes had avoiding pregnancy. This may support the contention that many abortions in the period were related to prostitution, but it seems too weak to support the claim that *most* were. See Olasky, *Abortion Rites*, 43–59 (quotation from p. 59).

48. Mohr, *Abortion in America*, 90–98.

49. *Maine Revised Statutes* (1841), chap. 160, sec. 13 (emphasis added).

tions needed to save the life of the pregnant woman. Moreover, at least until the 1850s, successful prosecutions for pre-quick abortions under this and similar laws were extremely rare due to the difficulty of proving intent. In light of the presumed legitimacy of operations to remove "unnatural obstruction of the menses," it was necessary to prove that the alleged abortionist intended to abort the fetus rather than only to restore menstrual flow.[50]

New laws, although still relatively lenient, began to be passed in other states. In 1845, Massachusetts made attempted abortion a misdemeanor and, if the attempt resulted in the death of the woman, a felony. However, the law was not very effective. "Between 1849 and 1857 there were only thirty-two trials in Massachusetts for performing abortions and not a single conviction." New York also passed new abortion legislation in 1845. Its law made no reference to quickening and took "the unprecedented step" of making women "liable for seeking and submitting to an abortion or for performing one upon [themselves]."[51] But this provision was never enforced against women in the nineteenth century. Mohr speculates that the aim of the law was to get at commercial abortionists and that the innovation of ending the immunity that women had had under the common law was due to belief that abortion was no longer limited to desperate unmarried women who were unlikely to be deterred by legal threat.

Michigan in 1846, Virginia in 1848, and New Hampshire in 1849, made abortion at any stage punishable, but provided severer penalties if it occurred after quickening. Other states and even federal territories passed anti-abortion statutes in the 1850s. The anti-abortion laws passed between 1840 and 1860 were, according to Mohr, "limited and cautious" responses to the increased number and visibility of abortions that characterized the period: "[O]nly three states struck the immunities traditionally enjoyed by American women in cases of abortion. . . . [A]nd thirteen of the thirty-three states in the Union by 1860 had yet to pass any statutes on the subject of abortion." Mohr writes, "The advent of more comprehensive and forceful anti-abortion laws throughout the United States still awaited a major campaign . . . on the part of a politically conscious organization with a vested interest in placing . . . less permissive statutes on the books."[52]

In 1847, regular physicians formed "just such an organization": the American Medical Association, aimed at professionalizing and control-

---

50. Platt et al., eds., "Survey of Abortion Law," 96; Mohr, *Abortion in America*, 41.
51. Mohr, *Abortion in America*, 122, 124.
52. Mohr, *Abortion in America*, 145–46.

ling medical practice in the United States. After writing and speaking against abortion on his own, the activist doctor Horatio Robinson Storer joined the AMA in 1856. A year later, at the association's annual national meeting, Storer urged his fellow "physicians to take a strong stand against abortion in the United States." The response of the delegates was to form a committee to draft a report to be presented to the AMA for adoption at a future meeting. Storer himself drafted the report, in which he urged doctors, through their state medical associations, to lobby state legislatures to enact strict prohibitions on abortion. The report was accepted unanimously at the AMA's 1859 national convention in Louisville. Says Mohr, "From the Louisville convention of 1859 through the rest of the nineteenth century, the steadily growing AMA would remain steadfastly and officially committed to outlawing the practice of abortion in the United States . . . , and the vigorous efforts of America's regular physicians would prove in the long run to be the single most important factor in altering the legal policies toward abortion in this country."[53]

The AMA found ready allies in the antipornography crusade led by Anthony Comstock. Comstock succeeded in having himself appointed an agent of the federal government with authority to censor the mails. He used this position to suppress the distribution, not only of pornography, but also of abortifacients and their advertisement.[54] He was responsible as well for the arrest of numerous abortionists.

The campaign to outlaw abortion was a complete success. Between 1860 and 1880, forty anti-abortion statutes were passed in the states and territories. The vast majority of these laws rejected the quickening doctrine and revoked the pregnant woman's common-law immunity to criminal liability.[55] By 1910, every state in the United States (with the exception of Kentucky, which reached the same result by judicial ruling) had strict criminal laws against abortion at any stage of pregnancy.[56]

There were both professional and political reasons for the energetic role played by organized physicians under the banner of the AMA, and perhaps for their success as well: Professionally, regular physicians were prohibited by the Hippocratic Oath from performing abortions.[57] Moreover, abortions were at the time extremely dangerous. Antiseptics had been discovered by Louis Pasteur only in 1867 and were

    53. Mohr, *Abortion in America*, 146–47, 154–57.
    54. Platt et al., eds., "Survey of Abortion Law," 99–100; Lader, *Abortion*, 90–92.
    55. Mohr, *Abortion in America*, 200–25.
    56. Platt et al., eds., "Survey of Abortion Law," 101–2.
    57. Mohr, *Abortion in America*, 35.

not widely used in surgery until the end of the nineteenth century.[58] Aside from surgery, abortion procedures used at the time "included blood-letting, taking strong poisons to induce vomiting, exercising violently, taking hot baths, pulling teeth, and using electrical charges."[59] The mortality rate for abortion was estimated at about ten times that of maternal mortality in childbirth.[60] In addition, science had shown that gestation was a continuous process from conception on, and "nineteenth-century physicians knew categorically that quickening had no special significance as a stage in gestation."[61] Marvin Olasky speculates that the success of the physicians' anti-abortion crusade after the Civil War was linked to the "solid anti-slavery impulses" of the era and the general repulsion at the loss of life during the war.[62]

In a more political vein, the period saw a great influx of Catholic immigrants. Because Catholics were thought less likely, due to religious scruples, to seek abortion, the Protestant majority—inside and outside of the medical profession—feared that birthrates among Catholics would outstrip those among Protestants and lead to a Catholic majority.[63] "There can be little doubt that Protestant fears about not keeping up with the reproductive rates of Catholic immigrants played a greater role in the drive for anti-abortion laws in nineteenth-century America than Catholic opposition to abortion did."[64]

Furthermore, doctors were extremely defensive of traditional sex roles and opposed the independence of women championed by feminists. It should not be forgotten that this era also saw the emergence of the so-called first wave of American feminism, signaled in part by the international meeting of feminists at Seneca Falls in New York in 1848. Many physicians believed that the willingness of married women to seek abortion was linked to feminism, which was leading women to reject their "traditional role as housekeeper and child raiser." Doctors

---

58. *Roe v. Wade*, 410 U.S. at 149.
59. Platt et al., eds., "Survey of Abortion Law," 94, citing Mohr, *Abortion in America*, 3–17.
60. Platt et al., eds., "Survey of Abortion Law," 98 n. 153.
61. Mohr, *Abortion in America*, 165. Luker contends that this knowledge was widespread among the general public (women included) and that the medical profession exaggerated the degree to which they were in possession of special knowledge in order, on the one hand, to improve their image as "professionals" and, on the other, to soften the condemnation of the many women of the "better classes" who were now having abortions: These women were ignorant rather than evil. See Luker, *Abortion and the Politics of Motherhood*, 20–25.
62. Olasky, *Abortion Rites*, 128.
63. Platt et al., eds., "Survey of Abortion Law," 99, citing Mohr, *Abortion in America*, 166–67.
64. Mohr, *Abortion in America*, 167.

repeatedly warned of "the growing self-indulgence among American women."[65] Writes Reagan, "The antiabortion campaign was antifeminist at its core. . . . [It] was a reactionary response to two important efforts of the nineteenth-century women's movements: the fight to admit women into the regular medical profession and the battle to make men conform to a single standard of sexual behavior."[66]

According to Luker, most doctors of the period believed that abortion was justified to save a woman's life and in other cases as well. Storer himself, for example, believed that abortion was indicated where there was fear of transmitting insanity or epilepsy to the offspring. Thus, "physicians agreed that the embryo's rights were conditional. What was at the core of their movement, therefore, was a *reallocation* of social responsibility for assessing the conditional rights of the fetus against the woman's right to life, both narrowly and broadly defined. From the late nineteenth century until the late 1960s, it was doctors, not women, who held the right to make that assessment."[67]

Ironically, as Mohr points out, most feminist leaders shared the physicians' opposition to abortion, though they did not share the physicians' explanation of its prevalence. Elizabeth Cady Stanton, for example, viewed the increase in the incidence of abortion as a result of "the degradation of women" in the nineteenth century.[68] Feminists generally thought that women had abortions because they lacked the ability to control their sex lives in the face of pressure from tyrannical husbands or because husbands, who wanted sex but didn't want the financial burdens of additional mouths to feed, directly pressured them to have abortions.[69]

In view of how many abortionists were female midwives, it is plausible that male physicians opposed abortion out of a wish to put control of women's reproduction in men's hands. In any event, regular doctors

---

65. Mohr, *Abortion in America*, 108. Interestingly, Olasky largely shares the view of many nineteenth-century doctors. He acknowledges that by the mid-nineteenth century abortion was no longer limited to unmarried women but asserts that the married women who had abortions were linked to the "spiritist" movement, which promoted "free love" and whose members Olasky characterizes as self-centered. See Olasky, *Abortion Rites*, 61–67. Mohr, however, citing the *Proceedings of the Tenth Annual Convention of the American Association of Spiritualists* (1873), contends that "[e]ven the so-called 'free love' wing of the feminist movement refused to advocate abortion." Mohr, *Abortion in America*, 112, 289 n. 90.

66. Reagan, *When Abortion Was a Crime*, 11.

67. Luker, *Abortion and the Politics of Motherhood*, 35 (emphasis in original).

68. E[lizabeth] C[ady] S[tanton], "Infanticide and Prostitution," *Revolution* 1, no. 5 (February 5, 1868): 65, quoted in Mohr, *Abortion in America*, 111.

69. Mohr, *Abortion in America*, 112.

had a financial interest in eliminating competition from these and other irregulars; licensing laws regulating who could practice medicine would not appear until the final decades of the nineteenth century.[70] "The specific cases of abortion cited in the medical journals almost invariably stressed that the performer was a 'quack,' a 'doctress,' an 'irregular,' or the like, and regular physicians remained openly jealous of the handsome fees abortionists collected for their services."[71]

Until 1967, when the first stirrings of legal liberalization began, abortion was a felony in forty-nine states and the District of Columbia (in New Jersey it was a "high misdemeanor"). In forty-two of these states, an exception allowed abortion if necessary to save the life of the pregnant woman. New Mexico and Colorado permitted it if necessary to save her from "serious and permanent bodily injury"; Alabama and the District of Columbia, to protect her life or health; and Maryland, for her "safety." Louisiana and Pennsylvania allowed no exceptions at all.[72] The result of these laws was not so much to eliminate abortion as to drive it underground. In 1936, an estimated 500,000 abortions—one for every five live births—were performed in America; in 1960, an estimated 1.2 million—one for every three live births. Of these 1.2 million, only a tiny fraction, about 8,000, were legally permitted therapeutic abortions.[73] Though the secrecy attending illegal abortions makes it appropriate to treat estimates of their number with skepticism, it does seem that a very large number of illegal abortions occurred during this period.

Movements toward liberalization began slowly. A small number of radicals pressed for legalization of abortion during the 1930s, but the association of this goal with the Left (the Soviet Union had made abortion legal in 1920) largely doomed the movement and led American

---

70. Platt et al., eds., "Survey of Abortion Law," 99; Mohr, *Abortion in America*, 160.

71. Mohr, *Abortion in America*, 161. At the beginning of the twentieth century, midwives were still performing about half of abortions, and regular doctors led a second anti-abortion campaign that was really an antimidwife campaign. This campaign had largely succeeded by the 1930s. See Reagan, *When Abortion Was a Crime*, 70–71, 81, 111, and 281 n. 77.

72. Platt et al., eds., "Survey of Abortion Law," 102–4 and nn. 178–82 (the statutes are listed in nn. 174–75).

73. Platt et al., eds., "Survey of Abortion Law," 105–6; estimate for 1936 from Frederick J. Taussig, *Abortion, Spontaneous and Induced, Medical and Social Aspects* (St. Louis, MO: C.V. Mosby, 1936), 23–28; estimate for 1960 from C. Tietze and D. Dawson, *Induced Abortion: Factbook* (New York: Population Council, 1973); estimate of number of legal abortions from Robert E. Hall, "Therapeutic Abortion, Sterilization, and Contraception," *American Journal of Obstetrics and Gynecology* 91 (1965): 518–32.

birth control advocates to dissociate themselves from the call for legalization. Major family planning organizations focused on making contraceptive devices and information readily available, first to married
women and later to single women. Their leaders often expressly condemned abortion and promoted contraception as a way of reducing its
incidence.[74] Advocates of liberalization directed their efforts primarily
at expanding the allowable legal exceptions rather than repealing the
laws against abortion. And doctors increasingly interpreted the existing exceptions liberally.[75]

According to Reagan, in response to growing female independence,
a new wave of repression of abortion started in the 1940s and coincided
with the "domestic revival" of the 1950s. Abortion was likewise a target of McCarthyism during that period.[76] With greater legal repression,
abortions became harder to obtain and more dangerous. Maternal
mortality resulting from abortions increased dramatically, especially
for black and poor women. "Public-health statistics revealed an appall-
ing picture of death and discrimination. . . . The illegality of abortion
had produced a public-health disaster—especially for low-income and
minority women. . . . Public-health activists interested in reducing maternal mortality now had to turn their attention to one of the most
important causes: illegal abortion."[77] Interestingly, Luker maintains
that maternal deaths from illegal abortions declined throughout the
twentieth century but agrees that they occurred disproportionately
among the poor and that they helped to mobilize some of the first
groups to enter the abortion reform movement.[78]

In 1952, a symposium of psychiatrists recommended a legal exception to permit abortions needed to preserve the pregnant woman's

---

74. Reagan, *When Abortion Was a Crime*, 37, 141–42. "Even the American
Birth Control League's *Birth Control Review* referred in passing to abortion as
'the murder of the unborn child,' and as late as 1939 Morris Ernst and Harriet
Pilpel [who became advocates of liberalization of abortion laws in the 1960s],
also writing in *Birth Control Review*, explicitly termed abortion 'the antithesis
of contraception' " (David J. Garrow, *Liberty and Sexuality: The Right to Privacy
and the Making of Roe v. Wade* [New York: Macmillan, 1994], 274; see 284–85
and 304–5 on Ernst's and Pilpel's later views).

75. Platt et al., eds., "Survey of Abortion Law," 107–8. Reagan claims that
this de facto expansion of the grounds for therapeutic abortion began during
the Depression due both to doctors' sympathy for their female patients' situation and to doctors' need to make up for their own declining income. See
Reagan, *When Abortion Was a Crime*, 143, 147, 158–59.

76. Reagan, *When Abortion Was a Crime*, 162–63.

77. Reagan, *When Abortion Was a Crime*, 214; see also Garrow, *Liberty and
Sexuality*, 274–75.

78. Luker, *Abortion and the Politics of Motherhood*, 73–76.

mental health.[79] In the 1959 draft of its Model Penal Code, the American Law Institute proposed a statute allowing abortions when two licensed physicians believe "there is substantial risk that continuance of pregnancy would gravely impair the physical or mental health of the mother or that the child would be born with grave physical or mental defect, or the pregnancy resulted from rape . . . or from incest."[80] However, it took until 1967, eight years later, for Colorado to become the first state to enact abortion legislation based on the Model Penal Code. In that same year of 1967, the AMA's House of Delegates passed a resolution urging that abortions be permitted under conditions like, though still significantly stricter than, those proposed in the Model Penal Code. Instead of two physicians' belief that childbirth threatened the health of the pregnant woman, the AMA insisted on "documented medical evidence"; instead of likelihood of grave physical or mental defect, the AMA required "incapacitating physical deformity or mental deficiency"; and to the exception for rape or incest, the AMA added that the pregnancy must threaten the woman's physical or mental health.[81] Regular physicians, now firmly in control of the medical profession, could finally afford to be tolerant of abortion:

> The medical profession organized to criminalize abortion in the mid-nineteenth century and to oppose those very laws a century later. The nineteenth-century regular medical profession had derived authority by proclaiming its moral superiority and positioning itself as paternalistic arbiters over female reproductive behavior. A hundred years later, the profession enjoyed enormous social authority. Yet as the abortion laws restricted and monitored medical practice, they undermined medical autonomy. . . .
> . . . 1969 polls found that the majority of physicians supported repeal of the criminal abortion laws and the majority of Americans, including most Catholics, believed abortion should be a private decision.[82]

In addition to the change in the status and outlook of the medical profession, and coming soon in its wake, a major factor pushing the trend toward liberalization was the new wave of feminism that emerged in the 1960s. Where doctors and public health professionals called for *reform* of abortion laws, new feminist groups began to de-

---

79. Platt et al., eds., "Survey of Abortion Law," 106; see also Reagan, *When Abortion Was a Crime*, 218.

80. American Law Institute, *Model Penal Code* (Tentative Draft No. 9, May 8, 1959), sec. 207.11.2.

81. Platt et al., eds., "Survey of Abortion Law," 108–9.

82. Reagan, *When Abortion Was a Crime*, 234; see also Mohr, *Abortion in America*, 256.

mand their *repeal*. These women insisted that abortion was a woman's *right*. "Abortion, they said, should be of concern only to the woman herself; physicians and other 'authorities' had no right to intervene." In 1961, after the failure of an abortion reform bill in California, women advocates of repeal formed the Society for Humane Abortions and engaged in leafleting, teach-ins, demonstrations, and even civil disobedience aimed at reframing the abortion issue as one, not about the discretion of medical professionals, but about women's right to control their lives.[83] NOW, the National Organization for Women, was formed in 1966, and "women's liberation" groups sprung up around the nation calling for women's sexual freedom and holding that "the state's enforcement of motherhood exemplified the oppression of women." Some more radical feminist groups, such as "Jane" and Service, learned how to perform abortions themselves and began administering the procedures without physicians.[84]

Luker speculates that a central explanation of the willingness of large numbers of women to adopt the view of abortion as a right lay in the dramatic and continuing increase in the number of women entering the labor force starting in the 1950s. Inability to control pregnancy meant that women had to interrupt their careers to take care of their children. This, in turn, meant that women could not accumulate the experience needed to advance occupationally and financially. For such working women, control over pregnancy would mean that they could have a career and approach economic equality with men. Luker notes that the American birthrate declined from more than seven children per couple in 1800 to about three per couple in 1900; the changes in the economy, she surmises, reduced the need for large numbers of children. She contends that, "[i]f the first abortion controversy [in the second half of the nineteenth century] was a reaction to the decreasing economic value of large families to nineteenth-century Americans, the second abortion controversy [in the middle of the twentieth century] can be seen as a reaction to the increasing economic cost of children to *women* in the twentieth century."[85]

---

83. Luker, *Abortion and the Politics of Motherhood*, 95–100.

84. Reagan, *When Abortion Was a Crime*, 224–29. According to Garrow, "Jane" started off as an abortion referral service, until some of its members inadvertently learned (early in 1971) that the male "doctors" to whom they were sending women for abortions were not real physicians! Learning this, the women's group dispensed with the men, lowered the fees, and began to perform the procedures themselves and to teach them to other women. "Jane" was performing about thirty-five hundred abortions a year prior to legalization. It experienced no fatalities. See Garrow, *Liberty and Sexuality*, 486–87.

85. Luker, *Abortion and the Politics of Motherhood*, 113–18, 125 (emphasis in original).

Three other causes of the trend to liberalization stand out. First, beginning in the 1950s and continuing into the 1960s, the civil rights movement and the receptive Warren Court focused greater and greater attention on the protection of individual rights. In line with these developments was *Griswold v. Connecticut's* recognition in 1965 of an implicit constitutional "right to privacy."[86] In *Griswold*, the U.S. Supreme Court found that a Connecticut statute outlawing the use of contraceptives was unconstitutional because it violated the right to privacy of married couples. Second, a new openness about, and tolerance toward, sex emerged in the 1960s. Third, the fetal deformities caused by the German measles epidemic of 1964 and by the use of the drug thalidomide received extensive coverage in the media. Of particular significance was Sheri Finkbine's widely reported decision to travel to Sweden in 1962 to obtain an abortion after learning that her baby would likely be born deformed as a result of thalidomide usage.[87] Writes Luker, "[W]ith the Finkbine case, what had been a trickle of public interest in the issue of abortion became a torrent."[88]

Numerous religious organizations joined the call for reform. A liberal Protestant magazine, the *Christian Century*, called existing abortion laws "barbaric and cruel" in 1961, and the Unitarian Universalist Association endorsed liberalization in 1963. In 1967, twenty-one New York clergymen formed the Clergy Consultation Service on Abortion, offering abortion counseling and information about abortion providers; by 1969, the Clergy Consultation Service had grown into a nationwide network.[89] In 1968, the American Baptist Convention recommended allowing abortion on demand during the first trimester of pregnancy, and the Unitarian Universalist Association called for abolition of all legal restrictions on abortion other than the requirement that it be performed by a physician. Conservative and Reform Jewish groups likewise favored liberalization.[90]

---

86. *Griswold v. Connecticut*, 381 U.S. 479 (1965).

87. Platt et al., eds., "Survey of Abortion Law," 107; see also Garrow, *Liberty and Sexuality*, 285–89. Olasky emphasizes the role of Finkbine's abortion in causing press coverage of abortion to move in a more tolerant direction. Olasky, *Abortion Rites*, 278–82.

88. Luker, *Abortion and the Politics of Motherhood*, 65.

89. Garrow, *Liberty and Sexuality*, 281, 291, 332, 364.

90. See Rabbi Armond E. Cohen, "A Jewish View toward Therapeutic Abortion and the Related Problems of Artificial Insemination and Contraception," in *Abortion in America: Medical, Psychiatric, Legal, Anthropological, and Religious Considerations*, ed. Harold Rosen (Boston, MA: Beacon, 1967), 166–74; Israel R. Margolies, "A Reform Rabbi's View," in *Abortion in a Changing World*, ed. R. Hall (New York: Columbia University Press, 1970), 30–33, cited in Platt et al., eds., "Survey of Abortion Law," 109.

The role played by the Roman Catholic Church is, unsurprisingly, more complicated. In 1841, the Catholic bishop of Philadelphia, Francis Kenrick, declared that no abortion can be justified, even to save the pregnant woman's life. "Two deaths, in his view, were better than one murder." In 1917, a codification of canon law decreed excommunication for anyone bringing about the abortion of a human fetus. Since that time, formal Catholic pronouncements have repeated this general condemnation of abortion even when necessary to save the woman's life. It was endorsed by Pope John XXIII, the Second Vatican Council, and Pope Paul VI.[91] Nonetheless, as the moves toward liberalization multiplied in the 1960s and after, important Catholic intellectuals, themselves opposed to abortion, called for abolition of abortion laws on the ground that the church ought not to use the state to enforce its moral views.[92]

For all of this, legislative reform or repeal of abortion laws proceeded only slowly. By 1970, four states—New York, Alaska, Hawaii, and Washington—had passed laws permitting abortion on demand, subject only to various procedural requirements, such as state residency in Alaska, Hawaii, and Washington, and that pregnancy be no further along than the twenty-fourth week in New York or than the fourth month in Washington.[93] Elsewhere, reform efforts were either stalled or defeated. On the eve of *Roe v. Wade*, most observers believed that hopes for further legislative liberalization were bleak.[94]

. . . to *Roe v. Wade*

On January 23, 1973, by a seven-to-two majority, the U.S. Supreme Court struck down a Texas statute—originally enacted in 1857—that prohibited abortion except when necessary to save the pregnant woman's life.[95] Writing for the Court, Justice Harry A. Blackmun declared in *Roe v. Wade* that the "right to privacy, whether it be founded in the Fourteenth Amendment's concept of personal liberty and restrictions upon state action, as [the Supreme Court felt] it is, or, as the District Court [had] determined, in the Ninth Amendment's reservation of rights to the people, is broad enough to encompass a woman's decision whether or not to terminate her pregnancy."[96]

---

91. Luker, *Abortion and the Politics of Motherhood*, 58–59.
92. Garrow, *Liberty and Sexuality*, 342–43.
93. Platt et al., eds., "Survey of Abortion Law," 110–11.
94. See Garrow, *Liberty and Sexuality*, 482, 495, 539.
95. *Roe v. Wade*, 410 U.S. 113 (1973).
96. *Roe v. Wade*, 410 U.S. at 153.

In affirming the existence of a constitutionally guaranteed right to privacy, the decision acknowledged that the "Constitution does not explicitly mention [this] right." However, Blackmun referred to "a line of decisions . . . going back perhaps as far as *Union Pacific R. Co. v. Botsford* (1891)," in which

> the Court has recognized that a right of personal privacy, or a guarantee of certain areas or zones of privacy, does exist under the Constitution. In varying contexts, the Court or individual Justices have, indeed, found at least the roots of that right in the First Amendment, *Stanley v. Georgia* (1969); in the Fourth and Fifth Amendment, *Terry v. Ohio* (1968), *Katz v. United States* (1967), *Boyd v. United States* (1886), see *Olmstead v. United States* (1928) (Brandeis, J., dissenting); in the penumbras of the Bill of Rights, *Griswold v. Connecticut* (1965); in the Ninth Amendment, *id.* (Goldberg, J., concurring); or in the concept of liberty guaranteed by the first section of the Fourteenth Amendment, see *Meyer v. Nebraska* (1923).[97]

As to the content of this right to privacy, Blackmun held that the Court's prior decisions "[made] it clear that only personal rights that can be deemed 'fundamental' . . . are included." Those decisions also

> made it clear that the right has some extension to activities relating to marriage, *Loving v. Virginia* (1967); procreation, *Skinner v. Oklahoma* (1942); contraception, *Eisenstadt v. Baird* (1972) (White, J., concurring in result); family relationships, *Prince v. Massachusetts*, (1944); and child rearing and education, *Pierce v. Society of Sisters* (1925), *Meyer v. Nebraska* (1923).[98]

At the same time, the Blackmun's opinion recognized that the existence of the developing fetus in a woman's uterus makes abortion "inherently different from marital intimacy, or bedroom possession of obscene material, or marriage, or procreation, or education, with which *Eisenstadt* and *Griswold, Stanley, Loving, Skinner,* and *Pierce* and *Meyer* [had] respectively [been] concerned." Consequently, "it [was] reasonable and appropriate for a State to decide that at some point in time another interest, that of [the] health of the mother or that of potential human life, becomes significantly involved."[99]

---

97. *Roe v. Wade*, 410 U.S. at 152. Note that here and elsewhere, where quotes from Supreme Court opinions make reference to Supreme Court opinions in other cases, I have abbreviated the citations to include only the title and year of the case. Fuller citations of many of these cases can be found in notes 110 through 117 below.

98. *Roe v. Wade*, 410 U.S. at 152–53.

99. *Roe v. Wade*, 410 U.S. at 159.

Blackmun expressly denied that the fetus is a person under the Fourteenth Amendment. He noted that the use of the term "person" in the
amendment and in the body of the Constitution appears to apply only
postnatally (for example, the Fourteenth Amendment refers to persons
"born or naturalized") and that the district attorney arguing for the
Texas statute had conceded "that no case could be cited that holds that
a fetus is a person within the meaning of the Fourteenth Amendment."
And, though the Court's decision allows that a state might have a legitimate interest in protecting *potential* life, the Court does not allow that
a state could assert such an interest *from conception on*. In support of
this restriction, Blackmun pointed to the wide range of moral and religious opinions about when human life begins and to the fact that "the
law ha[d] been reluctant to endorse any theory that life, as we recognize it, begins before live birth or to accord legal rights to the unborn
except in narrowly defined situations and except when the rights are
contingent upon live birth."[100] Thus Blackmun concluded, "we do not
agree that, by adopting one theory of life, Texas may override the rights
of the pregnant woman that are at stake."[101]

Although a state's legitimate interests in maternal health and potential life may interfere with the pregnant woman's right to terminate
her pregnancy, they may do so only in ways that can be justified by
appeal to uncontroversial facts and that leave the right fundamentally
intact. Thus, the state's interest in maternal health becomes compelling
only after approximately the first trimester of pregnancy, "because of
the now-established medical fact . . . that until the end of the first trimester mortality in abortion may be less than mortality in normal
childbirth." And the state's interest in potential life becomes compelling only at the point of viability "because the fetus then presumably
has the capability of meaningful life outside the mother's womb. State
regulation protective of fetal life after viability thus has both logical
and biological justifications." Putting all of this together, the Court
held, "A state criminal abortion statute of the current Texas type, that
excepts from criminality only a life-saving procedure on behalf of the
mother, without regard to pregnancy stage and without recognition of
the other interests involved, is violative of the Due Process Clause of
the Fourteenth Amendment." It further ruled:

---

100. *Roe v. Wade*, 410 U.S. at 157, 161. For example, though a fetus can be
bequeathed property, if it is "subsequently stillborn, the property does not
pass through the estate of the fetus but reverts to the estate of the grantor. If
the fetus is born alive and subsequently dies, however, the property passes
through his [the infant's] estate for distribution" (Platt et al., eds., "Survey of
Abortion Law," 151).

101. *Roe v. Wade*, 410 U.S. at 162.

(a) For the stage prior to approximately the end of the first trimester, the abortion decision and its effectuation must be left to the medical judgment of the pregnant woman's attending physician [in consultation with his patient].

(b) For the stage subsequent to approximately the end of the first trimester, the State, in promoting its interest in the health of the mother, may, if it chooses, regulate the abortion procedure in ways that are reasonably related to maternal health.

(c) For the stage subsequent to viability, the State in promoting its interest in the potentiality of human life may, if it chooses, regulate, and even proscribe, abortion except where it is necessary, in appropriate medical judgment, for the preservation of the life or health of the mother.[102]

Justice Potter Stewart, in a separate opinion concurring with the Court's decision, emphasized that the "Constitution nowhere mentions a specific right of personal choice in matters of marriage and family life, but [that] the 'liberty' protected by the Due Process Clause of the Fourteenth Amendment covers more than those freedoms explicitly named in the Bill of Rights." Stewart went on to point out that "Several decisions of this Court make clear that freedom of personal choice in matters of marriage and family life is one of the liberties protected by the Due Process Clause of the Fourteenth Amendment." Citing some of the same decisions mentioned by Blackmun, he continued:

As recently as last Term, in *Eisenstadt v. Baird* (1972), we recognized "the right of the *individual*, married or single, to be free from unwarranted governmental intrusion into matters so fundamentally affecting a person as the decision whether to bear or beget a child." That right necessarily includes the right of a woman to decide whether or not to terminate her pregnancy. "Certainly the interests of a woman in giving of her physical and emotional self during pregnancy and the interests that will be affected throughout her life by the birth and raising of a child are of a far greater degree of significance and personal intimacy than the right to send a child to private school protected in *Pierce v. Society of Sisters* (1925), or the right to teach a foreign language protected in *Meyer v. Nebraska* (1923)." . . .

Clearly, therefore, the Court today is correct in holding that the right asserted by Jane Roe is embraced within the personal liberty protected by the Due Process Clause of the Fourteenth Amendment.

It is evident that the Texas abortion statute infringes that right directly.[103]

---

102. *Roe v. Wade*, 410 U.S. at 163–65.
103. *Roe v. Wade*, 410 U.S. at 168–70 (Stewart, J., concurring) (emphasis in original).

Justice William Rehnquist dissented:

> I would reach a conclusion opposite to that reached by the Court. I have
> difficulty in concluding, as the Court does, that the right of "privacy"
> is involved in this case. Texas, by the statute here challenged, bars the
> performance of a medical abortion by a licensed physician on a plaintiff
> such as Roe. A transaction resulting in an operation such as this is not
> "private" in the ordinary usage of that word. Nor is the "privacy" that
> the Court finds here even a distant relative of the freedom from searches
> and seizures protected by the Fourth Amendment to the Constitution,
> which the Court has referred to as embodying a right to privacy. *Katz v.*
> *United States* (1967).[104]

Rehnquist's dissent focuses on whether the right to privacy recognized in *Griswold* applies to the case of abortion. The idea of applying
this right from *Griswold* to abortion seems to stem from a brief suggestion, in a 1965 *Michigan Law Review* article, made by Yale law professor
Thomas I. Emerson, who had successfully argued *Griswold* before the
Supreme Court.[105] Emerson's suggestion was first developed at length
in a term paper written in 1967 by New York University law student
Roy Lucas, who went on to publish the paper and to become an important figure in numerous legal challenges to abortion laws, including
Roe v. Wade. (Lucas said later that he had never really thought about
the issue until 1964, when his girlfriend became pregnant and he had
to help her obtain an abortion.)[106] And, in a 1969 article published
(ironically) in the Catholic-affiliated *Loyola University Law Review*, re-
tired Supreme Court Justice Tom C. Clark explicitly endorsed the ap-
plicability of *Griswold* to abortion.[107]

I think it is useful to note, however, that the majority opinion in
Roe v. Wade could have been stated without reference to a "right to
privacy."[108] Rather, as Justice Lewis Powell reflected some years later,

---

104. *Roe v. Wade*, 410 U.S. at 172 (Rehnquist, J., dissenting).

105. Thomas I. Emerson, "Nine Justices in Search of a Doctrine," *Michigan
Law Review* 64 (December 1965): 219–34; see Garrow, *Liberty and Sexuality*,
337–38.

106. Garrow, *Liberty and Sexuality*, 335–39. Roy Lucas eventually published
the paper in revised form as "Federal Constitutional Limitations on the Enforcement and Administration of State Abortion Statutes," *North Carolina Law
Review* 46 (June 1968): 730–78.

107. Tom C. Clark, "Religion, Morality, and Abortion: A Constitutional Ap-
praisal," *Loyola University Law Review* 2 (April 1969): 1–11; see Garrow, *Liberty
and Sexuality*, 372.

108. Though it is important to see that *legally* the decision could have been
reached without appeal to a right to privacy, I do believe that there is a *moral*
right to privacy that should be recognized *legally* by a free society. See my

"The concept of liberty was the underlying principle of the abortion case—the liberty to make highly personal decisions that are terribly important to people."[109]

What is crucial about the decisions cited by Blackmun and Stewart is not that they affirm a right to privacy as such, but that each decision establishes that some highly personal liberty is a matter of fundamental right, though not expressly mentioned in the Constitution. In *Stanley* (1969), the Court held that private possession of even legally obscene materials could not be legally punished.[110] In *Loving* (1967), which overturned a law prohibiting interracial marriage, the Court held, "Under our Constitution, the freedom to marry, or not to marry, a person of another race resides with the individual and cannot be infringed by the State."[111] In *Griswold* (1965), the Court affirmed the right of married couples to use contraceptive devices; and in *Eisenstadt* (1972), it broadened *Griswold* to apply to both married or unmarried individuals.[112] *Prince* (1944) recognized the freedom of parents to determine the upbringing of their children.[113] At issue in *Skinner* (1942) was a law authorizing sterilization of habitual criminals. In voiding it, the Court referred to the right to have offspring as a "basic liberty."[114] *Pierce* (1925) held that while the state could require parents to send their children to school, the state could not require that they be sent to public schools: "The fundamental theory of liberty excludes any general power of the State to standardize its children by forcing them to accept instruction from public school teachers only."[115] In another education case, *Meyer* (1923), the Court struck down a law prohibiting the teaching of modern languages other than English. The liberty pro-

---

"Privacy, Intimacy, and Personhood," *Philosophy and Public Affairs* 6, no. 1 (Fall 1976): 26–44; and my "Driving to the Panopticon: A Philosophical Exploration of the Risks to Privacy Posed by the Highway Technology of the Future," *Santa Clara Computer and High Technology Law Journal* 11, no. 1 (March 1995): 27–44. These essays are reprinted in my *Critical Moral Liberalism: Theory and Practice* (Lanham, MD: Rowman & Littlefield, 1997), 151–67 and 169–88, respectively.

109. Quoted in Garrow, *Liberty and Sexuality*, 576.

110. *Stanley v. Georgia*, 394 U.S. 557 (1969).

111. *Loving v. Virginia*, 388 U.S. 1, 12 (1967) (Warren, J., for the Court).

112. *Griswold v. Connecticut*, 381 U.S. 479 (1965); *Eisenstadt v. Baird*, 405 U.S. 438 (1972).

113. *Prince v. Massachusetts*, 321 U.S. 158, 167 (1944).

114. *Skinner v. Oklahoma*, 316 U.S. 535, 541 (1942) (Douglas, J., for the Court). The Court did not declare that all laws providing for compulsory sterilization were unconstitutional; rather, since procreation was a fundamental right, such laws were subject to a high standard of judicial scrutiny, which the law in question failed to satisfy.

115. *Pierce v. Society of Sisters*, 268 U.S. 510, 535 (1925) (McReynolds, J., for the Court).

tected in the Fourteenth Amendment, the Court said, refers to the individual's right "to contract, to engage in . . . common occupations, to acquire useful knowledge, to marry, to establish a home and bring up children, to worship God according to the dictates of his own conscience, and generally to enjoy privileges, essential to the orderly pursuit of happiness by free men."[116] And in *Botsford* (1891), the Court stated that "No right is held more sacred, or is more carefully guarded by the common law, than the right of every individual to the possession and control of his own person, free from all restraint or interference of others."[117]

In the companion case of *Doe v. Bolton*,[118] Justice Byron White wrote a dissent that expressly applied to *Roe v. Wade*:

> I find nothing in the language or history of the Constitution to support the Court's judgment. The Court simply fashions and announces a new constitutional right for pregnant mothers and, with scarcely any reason or authority for its action, invests that right with sufficient substance to override most existing state abortion statutes. . . . As an exercise in raw judicial power, the Court perhaps has the authority to do what it does today; but in my view its judgment is an improvident and extravagant exercise of the power of judicial review that the Constitution extends to this Court.
>
> The Court apparently values the convenience of the pregnant mother more than the continued existence and development of the life or potential life that she carries. Whether or not I might agree with that marshaling of values, I can in no event join the Court's judgment because I find no constitutional warrant for imposing such an order of priorities on the people and legislatures of the States. In a sensitive area such as this, involving as it does issues over which reasonable men may easily and heatedly differ, I cannot accept the Court's exercise of its clear power of choice by interposing a constitutional barrier to state efforts to protect human life and by investing mothers and doctors with the constitutionally protected right to exterminate it. This issue, for the most part, should be left to the people and to the political processes the people have devised to govern their affairs.[119]

As for White's claim that the Court in *Roe v. Wade* simply asserted its preference for a woman's convenience over a potential life, Blackmun made clear that the Court's preference is to protect a woman

116. *Meyer v. Nebraska*, 262 U.S. 390, 399 (1923) (McReynolds, J., for the Court).
117. *Union Pacific R. Co. v. Botsford*, 141 U.S. 250, 251 (1891).
118. *Doe v. Bolton*, 410 U.S. 179 (1973).
119. *Doe v. Bolton*, 410 U.S. at 221–22 (White, J., dissenting).

against a grave detriment: the costs imposed on her by an *unwanted* pregnancy. Note my stress on "unwanted." It is not the burdens of pregnancy as such that constitute the detriment in question. Pregnancy is not a disease, and, though it is burdensome to be sure, its burdens are often willingly, even joyfully, accepted by women who want to have children. However, unwanted pregnancy, going through morning sickness and all the other discomforts—psychological as well as physical—of carrying a growing life inside one's body for nine months against one's will, is something quite different. And caring for, or even giving up for adoption, the offspring one has involuntarily carried to term adds yet more distress to this unhappy fate. As Blackmun wrote in *Roe v. Wade*:

> The detriment that the State would impose upon the pregnant woman by denying this choice [whether or not to terminate her pregnancy] altogether is apparent. . . . Maternity, or additional offspring, may force upon the woman a distressful life and future. Psychological harm may be imminent. Mental and physical health may be taxed by child care. There is also the distress, for all concerned, associated with the unwanted child, and there is the problem of bringing a child into a family already unable, psychologically and otherwise, to care for it.[120]

Such factors as these amount to far more than what White calls "the convenience of the pregnant mother."

A Limited Defense of *Roe v. Wade*

The Supreme Court's decision in *Roe v. Wade* has been the target of much criticism by legal scholars.[121] In this section, I shall sketch out a principled rationale for the decision and indicate how this rationale has been confirmed by the Court in *Planned Parenthood of Southeastern Pennsylvania v. Casey*.[122] I shall conclude by pointing out how, for all their virtues, neither *Roe* nor *Casey* solves the moral problem of abortion. For that reason, neither provides us with a lasting and stable solution to the legal problem of abortion.

I do not claim that the rationale I shall present for *Roe v. Wade* was what the justices had in mind—only that it is a way of seeing the legiti-

---

120. *Roe v. Wade*, 410 U.S. at 153.
121. See, for example, John Hart Ely, "The Wages of Crying Wolf: A Comment on *Roe v. Wade*," *Yale Law Journal* 82, no. 5 (April 1973): 920–49.
122. *Planned Parenthood of Southeastern Pennsylvania v. Casey*, 112 Sup. Ct. 2791 (1992).

macy of the decision. The rationale is based on two ideas about the U.S. Constitution: (1) that it is a constitution of principle; and (2) that it is meant to protect liberty against infringement by the majority.

Legal philosopher Ronald Dworkin has characterized the U.S. Constitution as "a constitution of *principle* that lays down general, comprehensive moral standards that government must respect but that leaves it to statesmen and judges to decide what these standards mean in concrete circumstances. What the due process and equal protection clauses [of the Fourteenth Amendment] mean, on this view of the Constitution, depends on the best, most accurate understanding of liberty and equal citizenship."[123] Fidelity to our Constitution is not fidelity to the particular attitudes and beliefs in the minds of its authors but fidelity to the Constitution's ideals. One of those ideals, as stated in the Preamble to the Constitution, is "to secure the Blessings of Liberty to ourselves and our Posterity." But to secure liberty for posterity, that is, for the generations to follow, the liberty protected in the Constitution must be interpreted in terms of what is needed for each later generation of American men and women to count as free citizens—not what was needed in 1789.

Now, it is neither necessary nor self-evident that the interpreting of the Constitution must be done by the Supreme Court. Some, for example, have thought that interpreting the Constitution could be done by the legislature; others, that it could be done by the people themselves. This brings us to the second idea: Liberty must be protected against infringement by the majority. And since the threat to liberty comes from the majority, either directly or through its representatives (the legislature), neither the majority nor its representatives can be expected to protect liberty against that threat. It is for this reason that the rights in the Bill of Rights are basically limits on what Congress may do: "Congress shall make no law abridging the freedom of the press" and so on. Since the president is also elected by and thus a representative of the majority, this leaves the Supreme Court as the natural locus for interpreting liberty so that it can be protected anew for each generation.

With these two ideas—that ours is a constitution of principle in need of interpretation and that this interpretation cannot be left to the majority or its representatives—I think that *Roe v. Wade* can be viewed as a

---

123. Ronald Dworkin, *Life's Dominion: An Argument about Abortion, Euthanasia, and Individual Freedom* (New York: Vintage Books, 1994), 119 (emphasis in original); see also Dworkin, *Taking Rights Seriously* (Cambridge: Harvard University Press, 1977).

plausible and principled attempt by the Supreme Court to interpret the Fourteenth Amendment's guarantee of liberty as implying protection of whatever rights are necessary to say that contemporary Americans really are free, self-governing, citizens in light of current knowledge of the threats to their freedom.[124] My reasoning goes as follows:

The Fourteenth Amendment guarantees liberty, and we must assume that this is a real protection of something. If it is really to protect something, then we must be able to determine what the content of the "liberty" in the amendment is. All concerned believe it has content. Even Rehnquist acknowledged in his dissent that the liberty that "the Fourteenth Amendment protects, embraces more than the rights found in the Bill of Rights."[125] How, then, shall we determine what (else) is covered by this protected liberty? We could leave it to the state legislatures. But since the constitutional guarantee protects liberty against legislative majorities, that would undermine the point of the guarantee. For all practical purposes, the Court must determine the content of the protected liberty.

Since the Fourteenth Amendment is stated in broad and unspecific language ("liberty" instead of an enumeration of rights), the Court must take this as a principle or an ideal to be interpreted in terms of what is currently needed to realize the principle or ideal of liberty. Thus, liberty must include whatever rights are necessary now to say that people really are free, self-governing citizens.

Such rights fall into two categories: political rights and privacy rights. Unless one has control over one's political institutions and over one's private life, a person is not truly a free, self-governing citizen. The political rights are those that, in the words of Justice Benjamin Cardozo, are implicit in "a scheme of ordered liberty."[126] These are rights—such as the right to assemble and petition government, the right to freedom of expression, the right to due process, and so on—without which one cannot be said to be a free citizen of a democratically governed polity. It is here that much of the justification for using the Fourteenth Amendment as a means to make the rights in the Bill

---

124. Though this way of reading the Constitution requires some creative interpretation, I have argued elsewhere that it amounts to being true to the Constitution understood as a promise to citizens to keep government legitimate and nontyrannical. See Jeffrey Reiman, "The Constitution, Rights, and the Conditions of Legitimacy," in *Constitutionalism: The Philosophical Dimension*, ed. A. Rosenbaum (Westport, CT: Greenwood, 1988), 127–49, reprinted in Reiman, *Critical Moral Liberalism*, 123–47.

125. *Roe v. Wade*, 410 U.S. at 172–73 (Rehnquist, J., dissenting).

126. *Palko v. Connecticut*, 302 U.S. 319, 325 (1937) (Cardozo, J., for the Court).

of Rights apply to the states (which they were not originally meant to do, and which the authors of the Fourteenth Amendment do not appear to have meant to make them do)[127] might be found.

The privacy rights are those that protect people's freedom to make and act on extremely personal decisions. These are rights without which one could not be said to have sufficient authority over one's personal life to count as a free person. Consequently, in the context of *Roe v. Wade*, the so-called right to privacy is best understood as a shorthand for a number of rights that (along with certain political rights) must be taken to be implicit in "liberty" if that term is to have any real significance. Unless certain extremely personal decisions and the ability to act on them are protected from state interference, people cannot be said truly to possess liberty.

Of course, the decision whether to continue a pregnancy already underway is not a personal or private decision in the way in which, say, the decision whether to try to become pregnant is, because the former concerns a nonconsenting being other than the person making the decision—the fetus. However, since the legal and moral status of the fetus is highly controversial, to grant a state the authority to determine that status and build it into its laws effectively sacrifices the woman's liberty to the views of only a part of the electorate. Here it is important to recall Blackmun's statement: "[W]e do not agree that, by adopting one theory of life, Texas may override the rights of the pregnant woman that are at stake."[128] The Court thus recognized that any right can be overridden if a state may embody controversial theories in its laws.

This point is worth spelling out. As has already been noted, liberty and the rights that give it force are protections against what the majority of citizens, acting through their normal political processes, may do to individual citizens. If legislatures are unlimited in the theories they may embody in their laws, they are effectively given back just the power that the protection of individual liberty was meant to take from them in the first place. If, for example, the legislature is free to say what is and what is not a human life, it might define a sperm as a human life and then punish as murderers people who masturbate or use contraception. Or, as Dworkin has written, "[i]f a state could declare trees to be persons with a constitutional right to life, it could prohibit the publication of newspapers or books in spite of the First

---

127. See, for example, William E. Nelson, *The Fourteenth Amendment: From Political Principle to Judicial Doctrine* (Cambridge, MA: Harvard University Press, 1988).

128. *Roe v. Wade*, 410 U.S. at 162.

Amendment's guarantee of free speech, which is not a license to kill."[129] Consequently, the standard implicit in Blackmun's rendering of the majority opinion is appropriate: Where a presumptive fundamental liberty is at stake, no controversial theory can be used to restrict that liberty.[130]

This standard should not be confused with the idea that constitutional (or other legal) decisions should be made on neutral grounds. There is nothing neutral about the argument that I am making; it is squarely partisan in favor of liberty. Nor is the idea that the fetus is not a legal person any more neutral than the idea that the fetus is a legal person. If the fetus had been regarded as a person in our law for centuries, or if the idea that the fetus is a person were very widely shared, then Texas's theory would not count as a controversial one in the argument that I am making—though it would still be far from neutral.

With controversial theories about the beginning of human life or legal personhood ruled out, the decision whether or not to continue a pregnancy is effectively assimilated to the decision whether or not to start one, and it becomes the sort of personal right that has been protected in *Griswold* and the other decisions mentioned by Blackmun and Stewart. This is enough to meet Justice White's objection that controversial issues "over which reasonable men may easily and heatedly differ . . . should be left to the people and to the political processes the people have devised to govern their affairs." It is precisely because reasonable men (and women) differ "easily and heatedly" on the abortion issue that it cannot be left to normal political processes without jeopardizing a fundamental liberty. On this interpretation, the Court's decision in *Roe v. Wade* has more constitutional justification than Rehnquist's dissent grants, and it is certainly no mere act of "raw judicial power" as White asserts.

---

129. Dworkin, *Life's Dominion*, 114.

130. It might seem that this argument could be turned around in defense of the fetus. Just as a controversial theory of when life begins cannot be used to restrict a woman's presumptive legal right to choose whether to continue pregnancy, so, the counterargument would run, a controversial theory of when life *does not begin* cannot be used to restrict a fetus's presumptive legal right to life. However, the situation of the woman and of the fetus are not on a par. The woman's presumptive right to choose whether to continue her pregnancy is based on her undeniable right to control her body and actions—no controversial theory is needed to give her that. Unlike the woman, the fetus does not start with a presumptive right which is overridden by a controversial theory—rather, a controversial theory is needed to establish that it has any legal right to life at all. Consequently, the woman does—and fetus does not—have a presumptive legal right that would stand if controversial theories were eliminated on both sides. I owe the suggestion about turning the argument around to the fetus's advantage to David Luban.

In the period after *Roe v. Wade*, the Reagan and Bush administrations called upon the Supreme Court to overrule *Roe*. The Court did reject as too rigid the *Roe* trimester framework and allowed states to enact certain restrictions on abortion, such as requiring waiting periods, parental consent for minor females, and counseling. However, on June 29, 1992, the Court, in *Planned Parenthood of Southeastern Pennsylvania v. Casey*, reaffirmed the key holdings of *Roe v. Wade*. The majority opinion—announced by Reagan appointees Sandra Day O'Connor and Anthony M. Kennedy and Bush appointee David H. Souter—asserted that *Roe v. Wade* stood firmly on the Fourteenth Amendment's guarantee of individual liberty, and noted that, since *Roe*, "[t]he ability of women to participate equally in the economic and social life of the Nation has been facilitated by their ability to control their reproductive lives."[131] Reading sections of the majority opinion from the bench, Justice Kennedy stated:

> These matters, involving the most intimate and personal choices a person may make in a lifetime, choices central to personal dignity and autonomy, are central to the liberty protected by the Fourteenth Amendment. At the heart of liberty is the right to define one's own concept of existence, of meaning, of the universe, and of the mystery of human life. . . . [In abortion,] the liberty of the woman is at stake in a sense unique to the human condition and so unique to the law. . . . [In having to endure an unwanted pregnancy, her] suffering is too intimate and personal for the State to insist, without more, upon its own vision of the woman's role. . . . The destiny of the woman must be shaped to a large extent on her own conception of her spiritual imperatives and her place in society.[132]

In *Casey*, the Court rejected the trimester framework, holding that the state does have an interest in potential life even prior to viability; however, it accepted the notion that viability is the point after which (and only after which) the state has the right to *prohibit* abortion (if not necessary to preserve the pregnant woman's life or health). It also held that any restrictions that the state does place on a woman's right prior to viability must not amount to an undue burden: "[T]he means chosen by the State to further the interest in potential life must be calculated to inform the woman's free choice, not hinder it."[133]

As a solution to the legal problems, *Roe*, as modified by *Casey*, has

131. *Planned Parenthood of Southeastern Pennsylvania v. Casey*, 112 Sup. Ct. at 2797.

132. *Planned Parenthood of Southeastern Pennsylvania v. Casey*, 112 Sup. Ct. at 2807, quoted in Garrow, *Liberty and Sexuality*, 694.

133. *Planned Parenthood of Southeastern Pennsylvania v. Casey*, 112 Sup. Ct. at 2820, quoted in Garrow, *Liberty and Sexuality*, 697.

the advantage of making clear that the woman's right is not the product of some mysterious unwritten right to privacy but is, rather, the practically necessary implication of the U.S. Constitution's guarantee of liberty. On the other hand, by focusing on viability as the point after which the state has the right to prohibit abortions, the Court has rendered women's liberty fragile after all. Fetal viability is a function of medical technology. At present, it is determined by fetal lung capacity, which is not normally sufficient for the fetus to be preserved outside the womb prior to about the twenty-fourth week of gestation. However, it is highly likely that medical science will eventually figure out how to increase lung capacity at earlier stages, or how to preserve the lives of fetuses with less lung capacity, or both. Thus, "[it] is certainly reasonable to believe," as Justice O'Connor observed, nine years before *Casey*, in her dissent in the 1983 case of *Akron v. Akron Center for Reproductive Health*, "that fetal viability in the first trimester of pregnancy may be possible in the not too distant future." With this development, the state would have the right to prohibit even first trimester abortions, and women would lose the liberty that *Roe* aimed to protect. O'Connor was correct in concluding that "[t]he *Roe* framework . . . is clearly on a collision course with itself."[134]

The source of this problem lies in the fact that the Court did not try to settle the moral question of when human life merits protection. Without that, viability is no better than a temporary compromise. For the moment, it protects women's liberty (since almost all abortions are performed before viability, most of them in the first trimester), while according some respect to the views of those who would protect the life of the fetus prior to birth. Because, as Justice O'Connor observed, this cannot last, the abortion problem will be back to haunt us. Thus, we need a solution to the moral problem. I shall try to present and defend such a solution in chapter 3. But, first, in chapter 2, it will help to review the existing arguments for a moral solution and see why they fail to resolve the issue.

---

134. *City of Akron v. Akron Center for Reproductive Health*, 462 U.S. 416, 457–58 (1983) (O'Connor, J., dissenting), quoted in Garrow, *Liberty and Sexuality*, 643.

2

The Main Abortion Arguments
and Why They Fail

[A]ll complete human beings, human embryos or fetuses included,
are persons.
>   Patrick Lee, *Abortion and Unborn Human Life*

[A] fetus, even a fully developed one, is considerably less personlike than is the average mature mammal, indeed the average fish.
>   Mary Anne Warren, "On the Moral and Legal Status of Abortion"

In this chapter, I shall examine the main arguments about the morality
of abortion to see whether they work to prove either the moral permissibility of abortion or its immorality. I will show that they do neither.
However, this tour of the waterfront is meant to be more than negative.
As we see how and why the main arguments fail, we shall learn about
the requirements that an argument must satisfy to succeed.

Some writers have tried to argue for a moral position on abortion
without addressing the issue of the fetus's moral status. I shall start by
considering some representative samples of this approach. I shall try
to show that, though these attempts add important dimensions to the
consideration of the morality of abortion, they cannot settle that issue
without addressing the moral status of the fetus. That will prepare us
for a detailed look at the arguments, pro-life and pro-choice, that do
try to determine the fetus's moral status. Accordingly, this chapter is
divided into two main sections: "Arguing around the Fetus" and "Arguing about the Fetus."[1]

---

1. For an excellent overview of the various strategies used in arguing for
and against the moral permissibility of abortion, see Susan Dwyer, "Understanding the Problem of Abortion," in *The Problem of Abortion*, ed. J. Feinberg
and S. Dwyer, 3rd ed. (Belmont, CA: Wadsworth, 1997), 1–20.

Arguing around the Fetus

A Woman's Right to Control Her Body

Some people think that the right to abortion follows directly from a woman's right to control her body. This is a mistake because a right to control one's body does not entitle one to harm another person's body. Think of the common phrase "My right to swing my fist ends where your nose begins." What this means is that my moral right to control my body ends where your right to have your body not interfered with begins. Consequently, if the fetus is, as pro-lifers contend, a formal person, then a woman's right to control her body will end where it is about to invade the fetus's—another person's—body. To determine whether this is the case, we must answer the question of whether the fetus has a moral right not to be killed or perhaps even to have its life protected.

This comes through quite clearly in a recent article by feminist philosopher Alison Jaggar. In "Regendering the U.S. Abortion Debate," Jaggar recalls an article of hers, written twenty years earlier, of which she now writes: "I focused on the pregnant woman, virtually ignoring the fetus except to assume that its right to life was not so strong that abortion was always morally prohibited." Now she concedes that the argument she made then "for assigning women the legal right to abortion conceals more substantive moral and political assumptions than [she] realized twenty years ago. Specifically, it assumes not only that abortion is at least sometimes morally justifiable but also that making a morally unjustified decision on this issue is not such an indisputably egregious wrong as to deserve legal penalty."[2]

From here she goes on to address a number of distinctively feminist concerns, most importantly the issue of making access to abortion widely available, especially to poor women, "[i]n a society where women's heterosexual encounters are frequently manipulated and coerced and in which mothers remain primarily responsible for the welfare of their children."[3] Though Jaggar says that she still wants "to avoid the vexed question of fetal moral status,"[4] it should be clear from what I have already quoted that she sees that this is not completely possible. As Jaggar has already acknowledged, arguing for women's

---

2. Alison M. Jaggar, "Regendering the U.S. Abortion Debate," *Journal of Social Philosophy* 28, no. 1 (Spring 1997): 128, 130. The earlier article of hers to which she refers is "Abortion and a Woman's Right to Decide," *Philosophical Forum* 5, nos. 1–2 (Winter 1975).

3. Jaggar, "Regendering the U.S. Abortion Debate," 131.

4. Jaggar, "Regendering the U.S. Abortion Debate," 130.

control over abortion decisions assumes that fetuses don't have so strong a moral right to life as to make abortion always wrong, or so wrong as to justify legal punishment. For that assumption to be made good requires that the vexed question of the moral status of the fetus be addressed.

Viability

Some contend that fetal viability is the turning point, the moment when the fetus becomes worthy of protection of its life.[5] Viability is the capacity of the fetus to survive if it were removed from its mother's womb and placed in an incubator. The argument from viability might be understood as one that does take a position on the fetus's moral status. However, as I shall indicate shortly, the claim that the capacity to survive outside the womb changes a being's moral status is so weak that it is more useful to think of this argument, as the Supreme Court did in *Roe v. Wade*, as offering a way to avoid settling the issue of the fetus's moral status.[6] Though the Court ruled that states may not prohibit abortions prior to fetal viability, the Court did not declare that the viable fetus has a right to life. It held only that, from viability on, the state has a legitimate interest in the fetus's potential life and thus may prohibit abortion, except when needed to preserve the life or health of the mother. I believe that the appeal of the approach via fetal viability is that it offers a compromise position that matches many people's divided loyalties to the woman and to the fetus.

Fetal viability is not a promising candidate for when the fetus gains the moral right to protection of its life because it makes the fetus's rights hinge on whether it is dependent on another human being or not. We would not normally think that an adult who becomes wholly dependent on another human being would thereby lose what rights he had before.[7] But, if going from independence to dependence does not

5. For example, Alan Zaitchik, "Viability and the Morality of Abortion," in *The Problem of Abortion*, ed. Joel Feinberg, 2nd ed. (Belmont, CA: Wadsworth, 1984), 58–64.

6. "We need not resolve the difficult question of when life begins. When those trained in the respective disciplines of medicine, philosophy, and theology are unable to arrive at any consensus, the judiciary, at this point in the development of man's knowledge, is not in a position to speculate as to the answer" (*Roe v. Wade*, 410 U.S. 113, 159 [1973] [Blackmun, J., for the Court]).

7. "Viability, which focuses on technological factors independent of the fetus's development, is of no relevance in answering the deeper question of the moral claims of the fetus. Anybody might someday become dependent on a person or machine . . . , yet that would hardly make one a nonperson" (John Arthur, *The Unfinished Constitution: Philosophy and Constitutional Practice* [Belmont, CA: Wadsworth, 1989], 203).

change one's status as a bearer of rights, how can going the other way do so? Whether or not a fetus (or anything else for that matter) has rights depends on what kind of a being it is, what its special properties are—not on whether it is dependent on others.

And, in passing from nonviable to viable, the fetus does not become a different sort of being, just a hardier one. The changes that make for viability are essentially quantitative, such as stronger lung capacity; neonatologists normally estimate a fetus's chances of survival by its body weight.[8] It is implausible to think that such quantitative changes would change a being's moral status. And note further that, as Nancy Davis has pointed out, "a fetus developing *in vitro* is not dependent in the way that a fetus developing inside a pregnant woman is, but we do not suppose that the claims of the *in vitro* fetus are any stronger" than those of a fetus developing *in utero*.[9]

Whatever advantage the argument of viability gains as a compromise between the pregnant woman and the fetus is only temporary. Viability is a function, not simply of the fetus's level of development, but of that *plus* the level of available technology. Right now, viability is thought to begin somewhere about the end of the sixth month of pregnancy. But scientific advances will surely push this back.[10] There is no reason to think that we will not be able, one day not too far in the future, to remove a fetus at three months or two, and keep it alive in an incubator. In fact, there's no reason think that we will not one day be able to remove a zygote and keep it alive. When that day comes, if abortions are prohibited at viability, no abortions at all (other than those needed to save the pregnant woman's life) will be allowed. Women will have to either stay pregnant or submit to an operation. And, of course, someone will have to pay for the incubation of all the zygotes removed, not to mention finding them jobs one day. Sooner or later, we will have to determine whether the fetus ought to have its life protected.

---

8. Harold J. Morowitz and James S. Trefil, *The Facts of Life* (New York: Oxford University Press, 1992), 131–39.

9. "Nor is it obvious that we would take the claims of the *in vitro* fetus to be on a par with those of any other [post-fetal] person" (Nancy Davis, "Abortion and Self-Defense," *Philosophy and Public Affairs* 13, no. 3 [Summer 1984]: 206).

10. Morowitz and Trefil think that the twenty-fifth week is a kind of "wall" before which it is unlikely, in the foreseeable future, that we will be able to remove fetuses and keep them alive. See Morowitz and Trefil, *The Facts of Life*, 139–143. While it is true that, in the twenty-five years since *Roe v. Wade*, scientists have had little success in advancing the point of viability before the twenty-fifth week, the idea that this barrier is fixed for the foreseeable future strikes me as far too conservative in light of the unexpected advances science has made in this century. In any event, there is also the *un*foreseeable future.

Owning One's Womb

Some philosophers have argued that a woman's right to control her body gives her not so much a right to abort the fetus as a right to evict it as a property owner may evict an intruder or an uninvited guest. The best-known example of this argument is by Judith Thomson, who tries to prove that a woman has a right to have an abortion even on the assumption that the fetus is a person with a right to life. Thomson asks her reader to imagine this:

> You wake up in the morning and find yourself back to back in bed with an unconscious violinist. A famous unconscious violinist. He has been found to have a fatal kidney ailment, and the Society of Music Lovers has canvassed all the available medical records and found that you alone have the right blood type to help. They have therefore kidnapped you, and last night the violinist's circulatory system was plugged into yours, so that your kidneys can be used to extract poisons from his blood as well as your own. The director of the hospital now tells you, "Look, we're sorry the Society of Music Lovers did this to you—we would never have permitted it if we had known. But still, they did it, and the violinist is now plugged into you. To unplug you would be to kill him. But never mind, it's only for nine months. By then he will have recovered from his ailment, and can safely be unplugged from you."[11]

Asks Thomson, "Is it morally incumbent on you to accede to this situation?" She expects, and I do too, that you will answer "No." This is quite striking, since no one doubts that the violinist has a right to life. It seems, then, that a person's right to life by itself is no moral bar to your disconnecting him from your body, though this will result in his death. And it is an easy step to conclude that even if the fetus is a person with a right to life, a pregnant woman may justly disconnect it from her body even if this will result in the fetus's death.

Thomson's main point is that a right to life is a negative right, a right not to be killed; it is not a right to other people's services or to their resources to keep one alive. Therefore, if a fetus has a right to life, it would be wrong to try to kill it. However, the fetus's right to life does not give it a right to your body, any more than the violinist's right to life gave him a right to it. This argument will support using viability as a key turning point, since at that point the pregnant woman can assert her right to her womb without killing the fetus.

Thomson's argument is important because it is the closest we have to an argument for the permissibility of abortion independent of the

---

11. Judith Jarvis Thomson, "A Defense of Abortion," in *The Problem of Abortion*, ed. Feinberg, 2nd ed., 174.

fetus's moral status: Because a woman has a right to choose what happens to her body, she has a right to an abortion even if the fetus has a right to life. The argument has, however, some important limitations.

First, the conclusion of Thomson's argument will vary depending on how voluntary and intentional the pregnancy is. Thinking back to the violinist, if you had invited him to use your body, it would probably be wrong to disconnect him. Thus, the legitimacy of disconnecting a fetus will vary with the degree to which the pregnancy was intentional, that is, the degree to which the woman can be thought to have invited the fetus in. Pregnancy due to rape will be the most obvious case in which the pregnant woman has the right to expel the fetus. However, beyond cases of pregnancy due to rape or, perhaps, to contraceptive failure, things get controversial, and the argument yields increasingly contestable results.[12]

Second, as does the argument from viability, Thomson's argument skirts the hard question of whether the fetus does have a right to life. This is no criticism of Thomson; she intended to skirt this issue in order to make an important point about what follows even if the fetus is assumed to have a right to life. Nonetheless, her conclusion about the right to abortion is just as sensitive to technological progress as is the viability argument. We have no right to kill the violinist if there is a way to get him off our backs without killing him. Likewise, as science advances the date of viability, so will the period during which a woman has a right to an abortion shrink—all the way to zero, once a zygote can be removed and kept alive.

Third, Thomson's conclusion follows if we assume that the fetus has the standard, negative right to life. It will not follow if we have special obligations to protect the lives of fetuses that go beyond what we owe to violinists. In this vein, John Arthur asks, "[S]uppose you arrive at your remote mountain cabin for a winter of solitary writing, only to find an infant on the front porch. If we assume it's too late in the season to get the baby to town, can you then leave her outside to die, claiming that it is your cabin and you didn't invite the baby to stay?"[13] That most people don't find it easy to say "Yes" suggests that adults may

---

12. Frances Kamm has evaluated a dazzling assortment of variations on the Thomson argument and has tried to reach intuitively satisfying judgments about them, in *Abortion and Creation* (New York: Oxford University Press, 1992).

13. Arthur, *The Unfinished Constitution*, 199; see also John Finnis, "The Rights and Wrongs of Abortion," in *The Rights and Wrongs of Abortion*, ed. Marshall Cohen et al. (Princeton, NJ: Princeton University Press, 1974), 85–113; Baruch Brody, "Thomson on Abortion," *Philosophy and Public Affairs* 1, no. 3 (Spring 1972): 335–40.

have duties to provide more positive assistance to uninvited (even un-known) infants than is required by the standard right to life. And that might apply to fetuses as well. The standard, negative right to life may govern our relations with normal adults who can fend for themselves, while vulnerable and defenseless beings like infants or fetuses may have a right to our protection. Thus, as promising and powerful as Thomson's argument is, we still need to address the moral status of the fetus to resolve the moral question about abortion.

Virtue Theory

According to Rosalind Hursthouse, "virtue theory quite transforms the discussion of abortion by dismissing the two familiar dominating considerations [the moral status of the fetus and women's rights] as, in a way, fundamentally irrelevant." Regarding women's rights, she says:

> [S]upposing only that women have . . . a moral right [to terminate their pregnancies], *nothing* follows from this supposition about the morality of abortion, according to virtue theory, once it is noted (quite generally, not with particular reference to abortion) that in exercising a moral right I can do something cruel, or callous, or selfish, light-minded, self-righteous, stupid, inconsiderate, disloyal, dishonest—that is, act viciously. . . . So whether women have a moral right to terminate their pregnancies is irrel-evant within virtue theory, for it is irrelevant to the question "In having an abortion in these circumstances, would the agent be acting virtuously or viciously or neither?"[14]

To see that this conclusion is false, suppose that a woman does not have a right to abort the fetus, because the fetus has a moral right to protection of its life. Then, the answer to Hursthouse's question is, "In having an abortion in these circumstances, the agent would be acting viciously, in that she is acting unjustly, maybe even murderously." (Hursthouse admits that justice is one of the virtues, that is, one of the character traits needed for *eudaimonia*, a "good life").[15] This shows at one stroke that, within virtue theory, both the fetus's moral status and women's rights are relevant to the question of the morality of abortion. What Hursthouse has shown is that, if a woman has a moral right to abortion, that does not settle *all* the moral questions raised by any particular decision to abort—but this is a far cry from the moral rights being irrelevant.

---

14. Rosalind Hursthouse, "Virtue Theory and Abortion," *Philosophy and Public Affairs* 20, no. 3 (Summer 1991): 234–35 (emphasis in original).

15. Hursthouse, "Virtue Theory and Abortion," 229.

Hursthouse argues, further, that the question of the fetus's moral status doesn't matter because it is an assumption of virtue theory that "the sort of wisdom that the fully virtuous person has is not supposed to be recondite; it does not call for fancy philosophical sophistication, and it does not depend upon, let alone wait upon, the discoveries of academic philosophers. And this entails the following, rather startling, conclusion: that the status of the fetus—that issue over which so much ink has been spilt—is, according to virtue theory, simply not relevant to the rightness or wrongness of abortion."[16] Now, if this means that a person can be a good person without recondite knowledge, that is certainly true, not just from within virtue theory, but generally, since we normally evaluate people by what they intend to do, given either what they already know or what normal, reasonable people can be expected to know—none of which is recondite. But if it means that the morality of actions or the virtuousness of actors cannot be affected by knowledge that is currently recondite, then it is false. The reason is that what is currently recondite may, if it truly is knowledge, very likely become part of the knowledge that we expect normal reasonable folks to possess. Indeed, once we are confident that some important recondite views are knowledge, surely morality will require that we try to spread this knowledge so that it becomes part of common knowledge—and this will affect profoundly the conditions of virtuous action.

When, for example, Mary Wollstonecraft argued that women were as capable of reason as men and that they only appeared less so because of the restrictive conditions of their lives and upbringings, this was arguably recondite knowledge. That people could be deformed, truncated in the realization of their natural abilities, by prevailing social practices was itself a subtle (and, at the time, counterintuitive) idea that had only recently been introduced into European discourse. The application of this idea to women's situation was more radical still (and more counterintuitive). In light of this, a charitable feminist might say that men of Wollstonecraft's time could not be expected to have had this recondite knowledge and thus could have lived virtuously acting on beliefs in the inferiority of women. However, the truth of Wollstonecraft's recondite knowledge affected the moral nature of treating women as inferior, in that it implied that such treatment was truly wrong and thus that those who, unknowingly, performed it were mistaken *in morally fateful ways.* For this very reason, those who recognized the truth of Wollstonecraft's recondite claims were impelled to try to spread this truth until it became part of the common stock of knowledge that normally reasonable people are expected to possess

---

16. Hursthouse, "Virtue Theory and Abortion," 235–36 and 235 n. 11.

and act on. And, as this happened, it soon undermined the claim to virtuousness of those who continued to treat women as inferiors. This suggests that, while individual virtuousness or goodness may not depend on recondite knowledge, such knowledge is still important for current judgments about morality and, to the extent that it is confirmed as knowledge, it should eventually become part of what we expect people to know as we try to determine if their actions are virtuous and their lives good ones. It follows that, even if people now cannot be expected to know the moral status of the fetus, that knowledge (if it can be established as such) is important for correctly judging the morality of abortion now and, as that knowledge becomes more widespread, it will become important for judging the virtuousness of people's abortion decisions. Inside or outside of virtue theory, then, it is necessary to try to determine the moral status of the fetus.

Arguing about the Fetus

Human from Conception

Oxford professor of law and legal philosophy John Finnis provides this statement of the most common pro-life argument: "Every human being is entitled to an equal right to life; unborn children, even in the first three months of their life, are human beings (as any medical textbook shows); therefore unborn children are entitled to the protection of the law against being deliberately killed even in the first three months of their life."[17] Princeton political theorist Robert George accepts as well that all that is needed to establish the fetus's right to life from conception on is to show that it is a human being from then on. "At no point in embryogenesis," George writes, "does the distinct organism that came into being when it was conceived undergo substantial change or a change of natures. It is human and will remain human."[18]

---

17. John Finnis, "Abortion, Natural Law, and Public Reason" (talk delivered to the American Political Science Association panel on "Natural Law, Liberalism, and Public Reason," Washington, D.C., August 30, 1997). Finnis introduces this argument as a sample of the sort of argument that he thinks is unreasonably ruled out of liberal public discussion by John Rawls's notion of "public reason"—but Finnis is clearly sympathetic to the argument. Cf. John Rawls, *Political Liberalism* (New York: Columbia University Press, 1993), 212–54. I shall touch upon Rawls's notion of "public reason" at the close of chapter 3.

18. Robert P. George, "Public Reason and Political Conflict: Abortion and Homosexuality," *Yale Law Journal* 106 (1997): 2493.

To analyze this common argument, it will help to put it into more formal shape as the following syllogism:

Major premise: All human beings have a right to life.
Minor premise: The fetus is a human being.
Conclusion: Therefore, the fetus has a right to life.

It should be clear that this argument fails to distinguish between being human in the biological sense and being human in the moral sense; that is, it fails to distinguish between being a human organism and being a person. The only way in which the major premise is uncontroversial is if the term *human beings* in it is interpreted in the moral sense, as *persons*; and the only way in which the minor premise is uncontroversial is if *human being* is used in the biological or genetic sense, as a member of *Homo sapiens*. But if *human being* means something different in the major and minor premises, the argument is guilty of the fallacy of *equivocation*. That is, it is an argument that uses a term that looks like it has the same meaning throughout, but does not, such as:

Major premise: Flies have wings.
Minor premise: Pants have flies.
Conclusion: Therefore, pants have wings.

The human-from-conception argument proves its conclusion only if it assumes beforehand that because an entity is a biological human being, that entity is entitled to the same moral treatment—the same moral rights—granted to, say, human adults or children. But this is just what is disputed in the abortion debate. Thus the argument *assumes* from the start what it must *prove* at the end. This is called the fallacy of *begging the question*. An argument begs the question, when it takes as a handout what it should work to earn.

This, however, points us toward a possible corrective for this problem. If we had an argument proving that biological humanness is sufficient for (formal) personhood, then the human-from-conception argument would prove that fetuses are entitled to a right to life. Let us then look at two popular arguments aiming to do just this, the argument from *species membership and uniqueness*, and the argument from *potentiality*. Later in this chapter, I will take up a different and more subtle version of the human-from-conception argument, which I call the argument from *physical identity*.

Species Membership and Uniqueness

Start with the simplest claim, namely, that being a biological human being, a member of *Homo sapiens*, is itself sufficient reason to accord a being moral rights. Now, it is implausible to think that special rights belong to human beings simply because they are members of *Homo sapiens*. The view smacks of what some have called *speciesism*.[19] This term is consciously modeled on terms like *racism* and *sexism* and means, like those terms, favoring one's own group arbitrarily, for no good reason, simply because it is one's own. Mere membership in a species, ours or any other, is not an appropriate ground for moral standing.

Accordingly, we must identify something about our species—some property (it could be a cluster of properties) normally possessed by *Homo sapiens*—that is an appropriate ground for thinking its possessor is a person. What property does a *Homo sapiens* zygote, which is too small to be seen with the naked eye, possess that could give it moral standing? It does possess a full and unique genetic code that is, so to speak, the blueprint for a full and unique human being. (Actually, this has to be modified to take into account the fact that, up until the end of the first two weeks of pregnancy, a zygote or embryo may split into identical twins, which have the same genetic code and yet become *two* unique human beings.)[20] Why does a unique genetic code have moral standing? It is, after all, the sort of thing that gets produced all the time. Unique genetic codes are, to judge from the population problems in some parts of the world, all too easy to come by. Moreover, animals also have unique genetic codes from the moment of conception. Does that give them moral standing? Well, a pro-lifer may answer, it is the unique genetic code of *humans* that has special moral standing. But, then, we are back courting speciesism.

Suppose a zygote were conceived with a genetic code that is the blueprint for a human being who will have congenital blindness or a disposition to develop cancer later in life. Surely it wouldn't be wrong to alter this part of the genetic code if we can. But if we do it, we will have altered the unique genetic code and replaced it with a different one. And that surely means that a unique genetic code as such cannot have special moral value.

---

19. "That term, [*speciesism*,] coined by the Oxford psychologist Richard Ryder in 1970, has now entered the *Oxford English Dictionary*, where it is defined as 'discrimination against or exploitation of certain animal species by human beings, based on an assumption of mankind's superiority.' As the term suggests, there is a parallel between our attitudes to nonhuman animals, and the attitudes of racists to those they regard as belonging to an inferior race" (Peter Singer, *Rethinking Life and Death* [New York: St. Martin's Press, 1995], 173).

20. See, for example, Norman M. Ford, *When Did I Begin?* (Cambridge: Cambridge University Press, 1991), xvi-xviii, inter alia.

One writer, who effectively holds that having a human genetic code suffices to make a being a person, avoids speciesism in the following way. Patrick Lee starts by offering a plausible definition of (substantive) personhood and then claims that a human embryo satisfies this definition from conception on:

> A person can be defined as an "intelligent and free subject." Every intelligent and free subject is an entity whom we ought to respect, and whose good or fulfillment we ought to will for his or her own sake rather than treat as a mere means. By "intelligent and free subject" is meant, not necessarily someone who is *actually* thinking and willing, but the entity which has the *capacity* to do so. Someone who is asleep or in a coma is a person even though he or she is not actually thinking or willing.
>
> Human embryos have the basic capacities to think and will, even though it will be some time before they exercise those capacities; they are actively developing themselves to the point at which they will perform such acts. Hence all complete human beings, human embryos or fetuses, are persons.[21]

Thinking embryos? Though Lee does not mention the human genetic code explicitly in this context, it must be what he has in mind in saying that embryos have the capacity to think and will; they are, so to speak, programmed by their DNA to develop a brain and neocortex with these abilities. But it is quite a stretch to say that, because they will develop those abilities, fetuses have them now—"though it will be some time before they exercise those capacities." The point is that an embryo isn't simply *not exercising its capacities for thought and will*; it does not yet have those capacities. What it has is the capacity to develop into a being with those capacities. But this is no more a capacity to think and will than the capacity to develop legs is the capacity to walk.

Another writer who makes the same mistake is John Finnis. He states that "each living human being possesses *actually and not merely potentially*, the *radical capacity* to reason, laugh, love, repent, and choose *as this unique, personal individual*, a capacity which . . . consists in the unique, individual, organic functioning of the organism which comes into existence as a new substance at the conception of that human being and subsists until his or her death."[22] Laughing zygotes? Like Lee, Finnis has mistaken a capacity to develop the capacity to do X for

---

21. Patrick Lee, *Abortion and Unborn Human Life* (Washington, DC: Catholic University of America Press, 1996), 5 (emphasis in original).
22. Finnis, "Abortion, Natural Law, and Public Reason" (emphasis in original).

the capacity to do X itself. By such a jump in logic, the tiny cluster of molecules that constitutes the newly conceived zygote—smaller than a speck of dust, without feelings or thoughts (not to mention love or a sense of humor)—is magnified into a being with such moral clout that a woman in whom it has begun to grow has no moral alternative to letting it use her body for ninth months. I shall return to Lee's position later because he sometimes defends it by appealing to physical identity.

Potentiality

This talk of the fetus's genetic blueprint will suggest to some a different tack, namely, that what is valuable in the zygote is that it is a potential human child or adult. The fetus, even at this early stage, is a potential person, a potential bearer of moral rights. Thus, for example, Burleigh Wilkins holds that the fetus has a right to life "from the very moment of conception because it is a potential person."[23] Such claims appear to commit what Joel Feinberg has called the "logical error" of thinking that one can "deduce *actual* rights from merely *potential* (but not yet actual) qualification for those rights. What follows from potential qualification . . . are potential, not actual, rights; what entails actual rights is actual, not potential, qualification. As the Australian philosopher Stanley Benn puts it, 'A potential president of the United States is not on that account Commander-in-Chief (of the U.S. Army and Navy).'"[24]

Wilkins's attempt to get around this problem is more interesting than many because he tries harder than most to get clear on the meaning of potentiality. Importantly, he distinguishes potentiality from probability. Here Wilkins has his eye on John Noonan, who demarcates the fetus's candidacy for personhood from that of the sperm or ovum by the fact that the fetus from zygote on has a far greater probability of becoming a person than either a sperm or an egg does.[25] Against this, Wilkins contends that probabilities "might change drastically

---

23. Burleigh T. Wilkins, "Does the Fetus Have a Right to Life?" *Journal of Social Philosophy* 24, no. 1 (Spring 1993): 123; cf. Jeffrey Reiman, "The Impotency of the Potentiality Argument for Fetal Rights: Reply to Wilkins," *Journal of Social Philosophy* 24, no. 3 (Winter 1993): 170–76, upon which some of my comments here are based.

24. Joel Feinberg, "Potentiality, Development, and Rights," in *The Problem of Abortion*, ed. Feinberg, 2nd ed., 145 (emphasis in original). The quoted phrase is from Stanley I. Benn, "Abortion, Infanticide, and Respect for Persons," also in *The Problem of Abortion*, ed. Feinberg, 2nd ed., 143.

25. See John T. Noonan, Jr., "An Almost Absolute Value in History," in *The Problem of Abortion*, ed. Feinberg, 2nd ed., 12–13.

without affecting the claim that the fetus is or can become a person. For example, toxins in the environment might drastically reduce the chances that any pregnancy will be brought to term without changing our conviction that the fetus is or can become a person."[26]

Wilkins doesn't tell us why this should not change our conviction, but presumably it is because potentiality is a matter of the fetus's own makeup while probability is a function of the external competition. This is a tricky business, since, as I shall argue shortly, part of the fetus's makeup is its capacity to survive against the normal competition. For the moment, let's accept Wilkins's distinction between potentiality and probability.

From here, Wilkins goes on to distinguish potentiality from possibility, thinking that this will enable him to get around Feinberg's objection to the potentiality argument. A potential U.S. president surely does not have the right to command the American armed forces; but, says Wilkins, that is because what we mean by a potential U.S. president is simply anyone of a large pool of Americans legally eligible to be elected president—and that would be better described as a possible president. To get closer to the kind of potentiality that is claimed for fetuses, Wilkins proposes "the case of the medical student who is surely a potential doctor in a strong and relevant sense, i.e., he is well on his way to becoming a doctor. . . . Such a student has the right to participate in a limited way in the diagnosis and treatment of some illnesses under supervision of his teachers."[27]

Wilkins takes this to prove that beings that are "in a strong and relevant sense" potentially Xs have some of the rights of Xs before they are actually Xs. But the argument is too weak to prove that. Nothing in Wilkins's example of the medical student shows that his limited participation in diagnosis and treatment is his by right, rather than, say, because it is necessary for his training. And, even if the medical student has a right to this limited participation, it would not follow that he has it because he is a potential doctor. It is more plausible to think that he has such a right because he has actually mastered some of the techniques of actual doctors. Then, his right would be due, not to his potential doctorhood, but to his actual, if partial, medical competence. Consequently, Wilkins does not escape Feinberg's objection. That something is potentially (and not actually) an entity with qualifications for rights does not imply that it has those rights. Indeed, calling the fetus a potential person is pointing to a reason *not* to accord it the rights of actual persons.

---

26. Wilkins, "Does the Fetus Have a Right to Life?" 124.
27. Wilkins, "Does the Fetus Have a Right to Life?" 127.

But there is a deeper problem with potentiality arguments about the fetus, a problem toward which I have already gestured in mentioning the dependence of the notion of potentiality on that of normalcy. Wilkins's example of environmental toxins that reduce the probability of the fetus becoming a person, but not its potentiality, works only if the toxins are not part of the normal situation. If the toxins of Wilkins's statement were a normal part of the environment and fetuses rarely, if ever, survived them, surely that would change our conviction that the fetus is a potential person.

Consider the following. Suppose that, at the moment of the fertilization of a human woman's ovum, there is a mutation with the effect that the resultant zygote has the genetic instructions for producing all the parts of a human being minus only whatever was necessary to hold the parts together against the force of the earth's gravity. The result will be a zygote that would develop into a human being if it had been produced on a different planet—one with oxygen but weaker gravity than earth's. Here on earth, as soon as the cells multiply much further, they will be pulled apart by gravity and will not develop into a human organism. It seems to me that we would not think of this zygote as a potential human being. And all that it lacks is the ability to hold the human organism together against the external competition. This is what I meant in saying that part of an entity's inner makeup that accounts for what it potentially is, is its ability to survive against the normal competition. If that is right, then Wilkins's toxins do not subvert the fetus's potentiality to become a human being, because those toxins are not part of the normal environment. Thus, while Wilkins is right to distinguish between potentiality and probability, it remains the case that if the normal environment were such that zygotes did not usually develop into human beings, they would not be potential human beings.

It seems, however, that this is precisely the way the normal environment is: With nature left to run its course without human intervention, fewer than one-third of conceptions result in live births. Scientists Morowitz and Trefil observe that

only about 75 percent of the zygotes actually implant themselves in the uterine walls. Of these, only about 60 percent survive to the end of the second week of gestation. . . . [O]nly about 72 percent of pregnancies that have gone as far as a missed period result in live births. . . . In other words, if you were to choose a zygote at random and follow it during the first week of development, the chances are less than one in three [75% × 60% × 72% = 32.4%] that it would still be there at full term, *even though there has been no human intervention.* Nature, it seems, performs abortions at a much higher rate than any human society. It is simply not true that most zygotes, if undisturbed, will produce a human being.[28]

This undermines the claim that the newly conceived zygote is even a potential human being.

Finally, all this talk of potentiality bears the indelible mark of its originator, Aristotle, and his now obsolete worldview. To think that a zygote is a potential (substantive) person in any morally significant way makes sense only if we think, as Aristotle did, that the basic natural entities are dynamic beings, actively striving to realize their essential natures—rather than atoms and molecules.[29] Seen from the standpoint of modern science, a newly fertilized zygote is simply a tiny bunch of molecules. And it is incredible to think that a mere bunch of molecules, not yet visible to the unaided eye, could have enough moral weight to obligate a grown woman to stay pregnant against her will. Of course, adult humans are also bunches of molecules. But they are bunches of molecules that think and care and are self-aware. And, no doubt, a newly fertilized zygote is a remarkable bunch of molecules because those molecules contain the information and the mechanical impetus needed to bring more and more molecules together so that they will eventually become a human body with a human brain capable of doing the remarkable things that (substantive) persons can do. But, until the zygote's molecules do all this, they are just a bunch of molecules. They act blindly, if predictably, and they do no striving. Indeed, even to think of the zygote acting is a stretch, since acting suggests doing something on purpose, which a zygote cannot do. In short, I think that talk of newly conceived zygotes as potential persons reflects a subtle anthropomorphism read into what are simply mechanical processes. If this is correct, the potentiality argument should finally be laid to rest as a relic of ancient biology.

We noted in the chapter 1 that, for most of Western history, the anti-abortion position assumed, not that the fetus is a human in the moral sense from the moment of conception, but rather that, at some point during gestation, after conception and before birth, the fetus acquires some property (or properties) that entitle it to protection of its life. I turn now to consider three arguments that take this tack, the arguments from *what it looks like, sentience,* and *higher mental capacities.*

---

28. Morowitz and Trefil, *The Facts of Life*, 51 (emphasis in original).

29. "Aristotle wants to hold on to the metaphysical primacy of objects, natural objects, living objects, human beings. He does not want these to be mere configurations of more basic entities. . . ." (Michael Frede, "On Aristotle's Conception of the Soul," in *Essays on Aristotle's De Anima*, ed. Martha C. Nussbaum and Amélie Oksenberg Rorty [Oxford: Clarendon Press, 1992], 99).

What It Looks Like

Perhaps those pro-lifers who exhibit pictures of fetuses are making a what-it-looks-like argument. The political scientist James Q. Wilson certainly does. He proposes that we show people films of fetuses at different stages of gestation and that we outlaw abortion at the point at which the fetus looks like a baby to most people and engages their moral sentiments in its favor.[30] If this really were a moral test, however, one wonders why Wilson doesn't also recommend that we show people films of adult women at different stages of legally enforced involuntary pregnancy and that we permit abortion from the point at which the woman looks like a human being to most people and engages their moral sentiments in her favor. But, of course, it is not a moral test. Our emotional response to what things look like is, at best, a hint about what they really are and really are entitled to. To determine what things are and what they are entitled to, we must use our reason. Neither looks nor feelings will do. Surely this lesson was already learned in the struggle for the civil rights of black Americans, who were victims of discrimination based on what they look like and how that made other people feel.

Sentience

Sentience is the capacity to experience pain or pleasure, and it occurs in the human fetus sometime after the third month of pregnancy. Some scientists maintain that fetal sentience is impossible before the beginning of the seventh month, that "before the wiring up of the cortex [around the twenty-fifth week], the fetus is simply incapable of feeling anything, including pain."[31] In any event, the film *The Silent Scream*, which claims to portray a twelve-week-old fetus responding with fear to an abortionist's instruments, is simply fantasy in light of modern scientific knowledge. Fear, after all, is even more complex than pain, since it involves recognition of a threat and anticipation of its effect, something impossible for a fetus that, at twelve weeks, "has virtually no connections in its cerebral cortex."[32] What the film is more likely showing is the fact that before the end of the first trimester of pregnancy, a fetus will withdraw from unpleasant stimuli—but this is surely an automatic reflex, more like the turning of flowers toward the sun than like a conscious act of turning away.

---

30. James Q. Wilson, "On Abortion," *Commentary* 27, no. 1 (January 1994): 21–29.
31. Morowitz and Trefil, *The Facts of Life*, 158.
32. Morowitz and Trefil, *The Facts of Life*, 125; see also 158.

One philosopher who has defended sentience as the decisive property that makes a being morally vulnerable to murder is L. W. Sumner. His reason is that, since sentience makes a creature capable of enjoyment or suffering, sentient creatures have interests: "If the creatures we meet have interests . . . , we must grant them some moral standing. We thereby constrain ourselves not to exploit them ruthlessly for our own advantage."[33] On these grounds, Sumner proposes that we treat the advent of fetal sentience as bringing with it an entitlement to protection of the fetus's life.

Sumner's argument has the right form. He looks for a property of the fetus that justifies—provides a reasonable ground for—a claim to a particular kind of treatment. The capacity for suffering is surely such a property. Virtually all human beings know what pain is and think that pain is a good thing to avoid, and thus there is reasonable basis for a moral prohibition against inflicting it. The problem, however, is that that's all it's a reasonable basis for. The fetus's capacity for suffering is a reasonable basis for a moral prohibition against causing it pain, much as animals' capacity for suffering is a reasonable basis for a moral prohibition against cruelty to animals. However, in neither case do we have a reasonable basis for a moral prohibition against painless killing.

A person opposed to cruelty to animals need not be a vegetarian, though she should insist that animals killed for food be killed painlessly. Likewise, a person opposed to cruelty to fetuses need not be opposed to abortion, although she should insist that abortions be carried out painlessly. Since we have the power to kill adult human beings painlessly, I assume henceforth that we have this ability with respect to abortions, and I shall consider only abortions by procedures that we have good reason to believe are painless to the fetus. Such abortions are not reached by Sumner's argument.

Higher Mental Capacities

Moving further along the fetus's career, two scientists, Harold Morowitz and James Trefil, propose a biological definition of the *acquisition of humanness*, by which they mean the fetus's acquisition of those properties that distinguish the human species from other living things.[34] They suggest that "[t]he period corresponding to the onset of the functioning of the cerebral cortex (at about twenty-four to thirty-two

---

33. L. W. Sumner, "A Third Way," in *The Problem of Abortion*, ed. Feinberg, 2nd. ed., 84.
34. Morowitz and Trefil, *The Facts of Life*, 9, 16.

weeks) is a compelling candidate for the [fetus's] acquisition of human-ness."[35] One page after announcing that this definition of humanness is morally neutral, they declare that, in the case of a woman wanting to abort her fetus before it has acquired humanness, "it seems obvious to us that the presumption must be on the side of the woman—that the rights of a person who has acquired humanness must prevail over those of a fetus or embryo that has not."[36] Things get dicier once the fetus has acquired humanness. Then, the scientists say, "there is no longer a clear assumption of right on either side. In essence, the issue becomes undecidable from a science-based argument."[37]

It should be clear that the issue was never decidable from a science-based argument. The claim that rights accompany the biological prop-erties that distinguish humans from nonhumans is not a scientific claim, no matter how obvious it may seem to our two scientists. Fur-ther, that rights accompany such properties isn't obvious at all. Is it because these properties are *human* properties? If so, then we're back in speciesism. If not, then, it must be shown that possession of a func-tioning cerebral cortex is important or valuable enough, *and in the right way*, to justify having a moral right to protection of life. Well, a func-tioning cerebral cortex surely has great value, being the ground of our reason and language and all the rest of the distinctive abilities that make possible all the wonderful accomplishments of human civiliza-tion. But this is still not enough to conclude that possession of one is the ground of the human moral right to protection of life—and this is because of the unusual nature of the protection that we think humans normally have a moral right to.

Here what I have in mind is what I referred to in the introduction as the *asymmetric value* of human life. It should be clear that the property of having higher mental capacities does not account for this asymmet-ric value. However good it is that beings with higher mental capacities (or functioning neocortexes) exist, this great value is present equally wherever these mental capacities are present, that is to say, in any nor-mal human fetus after six months or so of gestation. One set of such capacities is as good as any other set (with respect to rights, that is, which are not given out on the basis of I.Q.). Why cannot one set be exchanged for another, then? If we destroy a human fetus and produce another human fetus, we will have just as much of these good mental capacities as if we had kept the first fetus with its set. Simply from the fact that our higher capacities are valuable, even extremely valuable, it

35. Morowitz and Trefil, *The Facts of Life*, 17; see also 119.
36. Morowitz and Trefil, *The Facts of Life*, 18; see also 154.
37. Morowitz and Trefil, *The Facts of Life*, 19; see also 154.

does not follow that these higher capacities have the sort of value that would earn their possessor a right to asymmetric protection of its life—that is, a right not to be killed and replaced by another human being.

We shall see that the requirement of accounting for the asymmetric value of human life is a very strict requirement, one that narrows dramatically the range of possible answers to the abortion question. Indeed, I shall argue in chapter 3 that it narrows it so much as to point us to the answer. Consider how the asymmetry requirement shows the flaw in another popular argument, the argument from *the conventional meaning of personhood*.

The Conventional Meaning of Personhood

Mary Anne Warren argues that it is personhood that warrants the right to life, and she seeks to determine if the fetus is a person. Warren understands a person (substantively, that is) as a certain kind of being and rightly notes that it is our normal practice to accord rights to that kind of being. What kind of being is a person, then? To answer this, Warren appeals to common parlance, and finds that persons are conventionally thought to be beings that have at least some of the following traits: consciousness, reasoning, self-motivated activity, capacity to communicate, and the presence of self-concepts and self-awareness. She contends that the fetus lacks these traits. Thus the fetus is not a person, and thus it does not have a right to life.[38]

What Warren has failed to do, however, is to show the appropriateness of valuing beings asymmetrically because they have the special traits that she links to personhood. Warren appeals to conventional practice, but that renders her argument simply a report of our common practice of awarding rights to beings with these traits, with no justification of that practice.[39] If the conventional practice of protecting the lives of beings with these traits is not justified, then we do not know that the absence of these traits in fetuses justifies denying them protection.

Therefore, Warren's argument is vulnerable to the criticisms raised against Morowitz and Trefil. The traits she identifies cannot be the ground of the asymmetric protection of life just because they are ours,

---

38. Mary Anne Warren, "On the Moral and Legal Status of Abortion," in *The Problem of Abortion*, ed. Feinberg, 2nd ed., 110–14.

39. This fact enables Jane English to stymie Warren's attempt by claiming that the concept of a person, as it functions in our actual practice of recognizing some creatures as persons, is too indefinite to "be captured in a strait jacket of necessary and/or sufficient conditions." See Jane English, "Abortion and the Concept of a Person," in *The Problem of Abortion*, ed. Feinberg, 2nd ed., 152.

for this would amount to speciesism. Instead, the great value of the traits themselves must be the ground. But, however valuable the traits are, they are equally that valuable wherever they occur. Then, why cannot a person with these traits be killed and replaced with another person with the same traits? If we do not have a satisfactory explanation of why it is possession of these traits that makes it appropriate to value asymmetrically the lives of their possessors, then we have no basis for denying that value to beings, such as fetuses, that lack those traits.

The Logic of Rights

Michael Tooley maintains that a necessary logical condition for having a right is having some interest that the right protects, and he contends fetuses cannot have an interest in staying alive.[40] A logical condition is something needed for the application of a concept to make sense. It is a logical condition of being a bachelor that one is a male above the age of puberty. If you spoke about a six-year-old boy or a sixteen-year-old girl as a bachelor, you would be misusing the term *bachelor*.

Tooley's argument is rather complex but comes down to this. In order to have a right to life, one must have an interest in staying alive. In order to have an interest in staying alive, one must be able to desire to stay alive. It is not enough that a being act in ways that contribute to its staying alive. All animals do this, and plants as well. Even machines can be programmed to keep themselves in good repair and thus to act in ways that contribute to their continued functioning. What these all lack is a desire to stay alive. That's what makes it generally acceptable to kill animals (painlessly), pick flowers, and junk one's auto.[41] To be able to desire staying alive, one must have the concept of oneself as a continuing self. That is, one must desire the continuation of something that one recognizes as oneself over time. This is surely more than a fetus can accomplish. (It is also more than a newborn infant can do, and Tooley faces the music and affirms that newborns

---

40. Michael Tooley, "In Defense of Abortion and Infanticide," in *The Problem of Abortion*, ed. Feinberg, 2nd ed., 120–34. Tooley has developed his view at length in *Abortion and Infanticide* (Oxford: Clarendon Press, 1983).

41. Not everyone believes that it is morally acceptable to kill animals even painlessly, but most people apparently do. Among those who do, most believe that, at least for animals more complex than flies and ants, there must be some legitimate reason for the killing, such as to provide food or to serve in significant medical research or, for some, for sport. These are reasons for which no one would think it is morally acceptable to kill human beings.

also lack a right to life. I shall leave this difficult issue alone for the present and take it up at length in chapter 3.) Consequently, fetuses are logically disqualified from possessing a right to life, and abortion is morally okay (at least in the sense that it does not violate a fetus's right to life).

As interesting as this strategy is, it seems to me to rely too heavily on the logic of the concept of a right. Tooley's mistake is not just that he effectively takes a fetal right to life as the only moral obstacle to abortion but that he imagines that we are so much the prisoners of our existing moral concepts that we need only determine what their logic allows to answer our moral questions. The fact is that we are not nearly so tied to our existing concepts and their logic as Tooley assumes. If there are good reasons for protecting fetuses against being killed and if our concept of a right does not fit fetuses, we need only create some new concept—call it a "quasi-right"—that gives all the protection given by a right but has only those preconditions which fetuses can satisfy. And, of course, even if fetuses cannot have rights to life, we might have a duty to protect their lives—as Stanley Benn recognizes.

Stanley Benn takes as a shortcoming of Tooley's argument that Tooley has not identified the logical presupposition of rights in a way that shows its moral point. Benn contends that that moral point is that rights protect agency. But he is still arguing about the logic of the concept of rights: "Like Tooley, then," writes Benn, "I am employing a presuppositional argument. I am arguing that to have a right presupposes not simply the capacity to desire the object in question, but to be aware of oneself as the subject of enterprises and projects that could be forwarded by choosing to exercise one's rights."[42] Since neither fetuses nor newborns are capable of this awareness, they are not agents. Thus, they cannot have rights, including the right to life. To his credit, Benn does not take this as implying that abortion and infanticide are okay. He recognizes that they might be wrong on other grounds. He even allows that we may have duties regarding nonagents.[43] Thus, Benn's argument leaves undecided whether or not we are required to protect the lives of fetuses, even if they cannot have rights.

But Benn's argument that fetuses are logically excluded from having rights because they are not agents is faulty. Benn recognizes that beings that cannot act, such as infants, have legal rights, though their rights must be exercized for them by some legal guardian. He characterizes this as an extension of the concept "by appropriate institutionalization to cases in which the usual presuppositions are only analo-

---

42. Benn, "Abortion, Infanticide, and Respect for Persons," 141.
43. Benn, "Abortion, Infanticide, and Respect for Persons," 140.

gously satisfied."[44] But if the presupposition of agency can be analogously satisfied by a nonagent, then the logical limitation of rights, legal or moral, to agents disappears. If legal rights can be possessed by nonagents, there can be no logical bar against—no absurdity or incoherence arising from—their also possessing moral rights.

What the discussion of Tooley and Benn suggests is that the question of whether we should give rights to agents only or to nonagents, such as, fetuses, cannot be solved by drawing out the logic of our moral concepts. If logic really barred us from applying some concept to a case that we otherwise judged worthy of that concept, we could just create a new concept to cover that case. But logic does not bar us, since we can always apply the old concept to cases that only satisfy its presuppositions "analogously," which is to say, not at all. The lesson is that the answer to the question of whether we should protect fetal life with a right to life or in some other way hinges on whether there are good reasons to do so, not on the logical preconditions of applying our moral concepts.

Continuity and Gradualness

Another line of arguments starts from the assumption that newborn infants are morally vulnerable to murder and argues that no clear, nonarbitrary line can be drawn between a newborn and a fetus. An hour-old infant is indistinguishable (other than geographically) from a fetus with only an hour left of its term in the womb. And even along the timeline of the fetus's development from zygote to birth, there are continuity and gradual change, not clear lines that set off one moral status from another. This, interestingly, leads to two different conclusions. Some take it to mean that the fetus at every stage has the same right to life as the newborn, from whom it cannot be nonarbitrarily distinguished.[45] Others take it to mean that the fetus gradually accumulates the features that make one a member of the class of formal persons and thus gradually earns the rights that come with that membership.[46]

44. Benn, "Abortion, Infanticide, and Respect for Persons," 142.
45. See Richard Werner, "Abortion: The Moral Status of the Unborn," *Social Theory and Practice* 3, no. 2 (Fall 1974): 201–22; Noonan, "An Almost Absolute Value in History," 9–14; and Philip E. Devine, "The Scope of the Prohibition against Killing," in *The Problem of Abortion*, ed. Feinberg, 2nd ed., 21–42. Note that many continuity-and-gradualness arguments are also physical-identity arguments, which I critique below.
46. See Warren Quinn, "Abortion: Identity and Loss," *Philosophy and Public Affairs* 13, no. 1 (Winter 1984): 24–54; Sumner, "A Third Way," 71–93; Norman C. Gillespie, "Abortion and Human Rights," in *The Problem of Abortion*, ed. Feinberg, 2nd ed., 94–101; Jean Beer Blumenfeld, "Abortion and the Human

The first group generally thinks that abortion is immoral at any time; the second, that early-term abortions are acceptable and that they grow less and less so as the pregnancy progresses.

A middle position argues that, until the possibility of identical twinning passes (about two weeks after conception), the batch of cells that constitutes the zygote or embryo is not yet a single entity that is identical to any future human individual. On this view, "aborting" the fetus prior to the fifteenth day of pregnancy is not abortion at all but contraception.[47]

The problem with all these arguments, whether they come out for early abortions or none at all, is that they start with the assumption that newborn infants have the moral right to protection of their life. This is a fair enough assumption in the context of the public abortion debate, since virtually no party in the public debate questions it. However, many serious philosophers have expressed doubt that newborns have a moral right to protection of their life. Thus, philosophers cannot simply take this for granted as an uncontroversial assumption—even if it is uncontroversial in the context of the public abortion debate. And this is true of nonphilosophers as well, as long as they are trying to find out what is right here, not merely what is commonly assumed in society. Moreover, unless we know *why* humans are ever entitled to the right, we can never know *when* they become so entitled. And, without that, we can never resolve the abortion issue.

Intrinsic Values, Intentions, and Double Effects

I turn now to an argument that stems at least from Saint Thomas Aquinas and that has shaped much of the Roman Catholic position on the abortion issue. With some simplification, the position is this. Some things are intrinsically good, and innocent human life is one of them. It is evil to directly intend to destroy what is intrinsically good, even as a means to produce something else good or even better. This is enough to rule out just about any abortion. This same view about the wrongness of intentionally destroying intrinsically good things underlies the so-called doctrine of double effect, which plays an important role in Catholic thinking on abortion to save a pregnant woman's life (and, for that matter, on the question of injury to noncombatants resulting from military bombardment).

Brain," *Philosophical Studies* 32, no. 3 (October 1977): 251–68; and Michael Lockwood, "Warnock versus Powell (and Harradine): When Does Potentiality Count?" *Bioethics* 2, no. 3 (1988): 187–213.

47. See Ford, *When Did I Begin?* for a scientifically informed philosophical defense of this view.

According to the doctrine of double effect, while it is always wrong to directly intend to destroy innocent human life, even to save one or more other innocent human lives, it is morally acceptable to do something to save lives that will have the expected but unintended result of destroying life. On this teaching, it is wrong to try to kill a fetus in order to save the pregnant woman's life. This prohibits, for example, the practice of craniotomy (crushing of the fetus's skull) which, before the advent of safe caesarian sections, was used when a fetus's head had grown so large that vaginal delivery threatened the pregnant woman's life. Even if craniotomy were necessary to save the woman's life, according to the doctrine of double effect it would be wrong because it involves directly intending to kill the fetus. On the other hand, it is morally acceptable to give the pregnant woman medicine needed to save her life, even if it is known that the medicine will kill the fetus. Here the intention is simply to medicate the woman, not to kill the fetus.[48] (The reader shouldn't have any trouble figuring out how this teaching would affect the question of collateral bombing casualties in war.)

One thing that is quite interesting about this view is that it does appear to provide a possible solution to the puzzle about the asymmetric value of human life. If innocent human life has intrinsic value and if it is always wrong to directly intend to destroy what has intrinsic value, even in order to produce equal or greater value, then destroying one innocent human life can never be made good by replacing that one with another or even with several other ones. Innocent human life will be entitled to asymmetric protection. Likewise, killing a human being will be intrinsically evil, without the implication that refraining from procreating is equally evil.

However, there are two weak points in this argument. The first has to do with the notion of intrinsic value, and the second with the distinction between intended and (merely) expected consequences. Many writers assert that possession of intrinsic value entails possession of asymmetric value—that it is wrong to destroy entities with intrinsic value even if one replaces them with as many or more other entities with intrinsic value. However, arguments for, or explanations of, this

---

48. It is, no doubt, ironic that Judith Thomson, in the argument considered earlier in this chapter, turns the doctrine of double effect around to support the right of abortion. If the fetus has a right to life, she argues in effect, one does not have the right to intend to kill it. But, if what a pregnant woman intends is to exercise her right to decide what gets connected to her body, she may act on this intention and evict the fetus even if an expected effect of that is the fetus's death, or even if the only way to evict the fetus is to kill it. Thomson, "A Defense of Abortion."

link are hard to come by. Merely waving at intrinsic value is not enough to do the trick. And, of course, one cannot solve this problem by defining *intrinsic value* to mean asymmetric value. That would not explain how having intrinsic value implies having asymmetric value; it would only assert that it does.

Consider that if one thing with intrinsic value is destroyed and replaced by another, there is no net loss in intrinsic value. If it is replaced by two intrinsically valuable things, there is a net gain in intrinsic value. This might be countered by saying that things of intrinsic value cannot be added up so that two intrinsically valuable things have more intrinsic value than one intrinsically valuable thing. But this is simply an unargued assertion, and, further, it is contrary to common sense, which normally assumes, for example, that murder of several victims is worse than murder of one and thus that there can be greater and lesser losses of intrinsic value. If the intrinsic value of human lives can be, so to speak, added up, then the intrinsic value of one human being is commensurable with that of another. And, if that is so, intrinsic value cannot explain why it is not okay to kill one human being and replace her with another one. In short, intrinsic value is invoked because it is thought to imply (or equal) asymmetric value, but no argument proves this and it is implausible to think that any will.

Quite the same applies to the notion that human beings are ends-in-themselves. An *end-in-itself* is an entity with intrinsic value in that it has value because of its nature and without having to serve any purpose beyond itself. Ends-in-themselves are thought to have asymmetric value. Immanuel Kant, for example, says that an end-in-itself "is one for which there can be substituted no other end."[49] Kant, however, gives no argument for this, especially not for the idea that an end-in-itself cannot be substituted for by another end-in-itself.[50] Later, when I suggest what property of human beings accounts for their asymmetric value, we shall see that having that property is plausibly described as a way of being an end-in-itself. But that will require us to go beyond

---

49. Immanuel Kant, *Groundwork of the Metaphysics of Morals*, trans. James W. Ellington (Indianapolis, IN: Hackett, 1981; originally published 1785), 36. For an illuminating account of Kant's claims about ends-in-themselves and their relationship to his overall philosophical vision, see Thomas W. Pogge, "Kant on Ends and the Meaning of Life," in *Reclaiming the History of Ethics: Essays for John Rawls*, ed. A. Reath, B. Herman, and C. Korsgaard (New York: Cambridge University Press, 1997), 361–87.

50. "The Kant of the *Groundwork* . . . supposes that we can see that reason and only reason can be an end in itself, but . . . suggests no way of deducing that from any more evident premise" (Paul Guyer, "The Possibility of the Categorical Imperative," in *Kant's Groundwork of the Metaphysics of Morals: Critical Essays*, ed. Paul Guyer [Lanham, MD: Rowman & Littlefield, 1998], 231).

the general assertion that something is an end-in-itself to a far more specific account. For the present, however, our conclusion is that being an end-in-itself—or its equivalent, a thing with intrinsic value—does not account for a right to asymmetric protection.

It might seem that such a right is accounted for by the other part of the doctrine of double effect, namely, that it is always evil to directly intend the destruction of what has intrinsic value, even in order to save (or bring into existence) other things of intrinsic value. Consider, then, the argument for this central claim of the doctrine of double effect: We normally judge persons good or evil by what they intend to do, not merely by what they happen to accomplish. This leads to the notion that states of mind are the real target of moral evaluation, and it supports the idea that intending to destroy what is intrinsically good is intrinsically evil. Having the intention to destroy what is intrinsically good is having an inherently evil state of mind. Then, supposing that innocent human beings are intrinsically valuable, it will be wrong to kill innocent humans even if we replace them with other ones, because it will be wrong to directly intend to kill an innocent human being, *no matter what else follows*. Thus, this will account for asymmetry.

However, this argument leads to unacceptable outcomes that render the doctrine of double effect extremely doubtful. One such outcome is seen in what Gregory Kavka calls "Extra Death cases":

> When an abortion can save the mother's life, but both mother and fetus will die if [an abortion] is not performed, we have an Extra Death case. The fetus perishes whatever is done, but aborting saves the mother. Yet the absolute prohibition view [that holds, as does the doctrine of double effect, that it is always evil to intend to kill innocent human life, *no matter what else follows*] says—quite implausibly—that we must not abort, that we must sacrifice the mother's life, even though the fetus cannot benefit."[51]

The doctrine of double effect makes a fetish out of avoiding the physical act of taking life, to the point that it is willing to sacrifice mother and fetus to this fetish. Indeed, this suggests that the doctrine is more concerned to avoid killing than to protect life, which implies that its prohibition on killing has lost its connection to what makes such a prohibition plausible in the first place.

It might be thought that one could simply exempt extra death cases from the reach of the doctrine of double effect by saying that the doctrine applies only to choices between saving the fetus or the pregnant woman. Then it will be acceptable to kill the fetus to save the woman

---

51. Gregory S. Kavka, "Banning Euthanasia," in *Contemporary Moral Issues*, ed. Lawrence M. Hinman (Upper Saddle River, NJ: Prentice Hall, 1996), 139.

if otherwise both would die. This would bring the doctrine closer to most people's moral intuitions, but at the cost of cutting the ground of the doctrine out from under it. Once it is granted that it is moral to kill the fetus to save the woman if otherwise both would die, the notion that it is inherently wrong to directly intend to kill an innocent being to save another is abandoned.

Philippa Foot has argued that the wrongness of killing humans goes further than intended consequences reach—as these are understood by the doctrine of double effect. She maintains that, to save five people, it would be wrong to use a certain gas in surgery, knowing that the gas will seep next door and kill someone else.[52] If that is so, it shows that the rigid distinction between intended and expected consequences is an artificial one corresponding to no real moral boundary. We are responsible for what we know we are making happen. If we get excused for making some evil happen, it will be because of all the elements of what we bring about, in light of their real moral weight and of the possible alternatives—not because the evil was not intended but only expected.

What is really wrong with the doctrine of double effect and the related teachings is that they force a distorting foreshortening of the moral field of vision. If, intending to kill the fetus, I am only allowed to look at the immediate aim of my action (ending the fetus's life), then (if fetal life is intrinsically valuable) it does seem as if my action is evil and my intention with it. But, if I am allowed to look at the whole picture and see that I am not just killing the fetus but saving the pregnant woman, then my action takes on a different cast. One who thinks that it is legitimate to kill a fetus in order to save a pregnant woman's life may think that the fetus's life is intrinsically good. He may, nonetheless, believe that destroying the intrinsically good fetal life in order to preserve something of comparable value is not evil. But, then, his intention to-kill-the-fetus-in-order-to-save-the-woman, taken as a whole, is not to do evil at all but to do good. And then he does not have an evil state of mind.

This is not to say that one is entitled to go around killing people for some greater good and then to justify it by looking at the whole picture with its net gains and so on. The point is that, if I am not entitled to go around killing people for some greater good, then that must be because people have asymmetric value—not because I am constrained to a moral nearsightedness that forces me, in judging my actions, to look

---

52. Philippa Foot, "The Problem of Abortion and the Doctrine of Double Effect," *Virtues and Vices* (Berkeley, CA: University of California Press, 1978), 19–32.

only at the act of killing those people and at nothing beyond that. Rather, if people have asymmetric value that makes it wrong to secure greater good by sacrificing them, that is something that I will see precisely by evaluating the whole picture in light of what is valuable in it.

Physical Identity

By "physical identity," I mean the sameness of an enduring thing over the whole period of its existence, as indicated by physical factors—cohesion of parts, continuous location in space, gradualness of change, and so on. So, if a newly conceived fetus and a fully developed adult are temporal phases of a single physically continuous entity, then fetus and adult are physically identical. I call this *physical* to distinguish it from *moral identity*, by which I mean the fact (when it is a fact) that a being with a moral standing at a certain temporal point in its existence has the same moral standing at some other temporal point in its existence. The general form of the physical-identity argument against abortion is that, if a being has basic moral rights at some specific moment of its existence (say, when it is a human adult), then it must have those rights at every other moment of its existence as the same physical entity (say, when it is a fetus), since at every one of those other moments it is identical to the being that has the rights. The claim, in short, is that physical identity implies moral identity. I shall show that this claim is false.

In the subsection titled "Species Membership and Uniqueness," I dealt with Patrick Lee's claim that a fetus is intelligent and free because it possesses the genetic capacity for thought and will, but I promised to return to Lee, as he also defends his anti-abortion position by appeal to the argument from physical identity. Note, for clarity's sake, how these two arguments of Lee's differ. The first claims that the fetus already possesses the traits that make it a moral person; the second, that, even if the fetus does not already possess those traits, it is a moral person because it is physically identical to the being that will possess those traits. So, for example, after criticizing L. W. Sumner's proposal that the advent of sentience gives the fetus moral standing, Lee contends, "[E]ven if sentience were the criterion of moral worth, it would remain true that [even before they are sentient] human embryos or fetuses have intrinsic worth, because they are identical with entities who at a later time possess actual sentience." And, more generally:

[A] human person is an intelligent and free, living, organic body. Thus, being an organism is part of what the human person is [essentially], as opposed to a property it has. As a consequence, the organism which a

person is cannot come to be or cease to be at a different time than the
time at which the person comes to be or ceases to be. . . . Hence all human
beings, including human embryos or fetuses, are persons [and thus it is
wrong to intentionally kill them].[53]

The argument seems to be this. A human being is essentially a (substantive) person, an intelligent, free, living organism. Since being an
organism is part of the essence of personhood, the organism that a
person is, is inseparable from that personhood, and vice versa. Consequently, as long as a human being is a continuous physical organism,
she must also be a person. And if it is wrong to kill persons, then it is
wrong, because they are persons, to kill human organisms, including
fetuses.

Underlying this argument, I believe, is the idea that, if an entity has
an essential nature, then it must have that essential nature for the
whole duration of its existence as the same continuous entity. It seems
to follow that, if the fetus is a phase of the same continuous entity that
is eventually recognized as morally worthy due to its essential nature,
the fetus must have that essential moral worth as well, and all the
rights and privileges that accompany it.[54] This is the argument from
physical identity.

But note that the traits that make a human organism a (substantive)
person are not present for the full time that the human organism exists.
It follows that, if fetuses never developed properties beyond those that
they have during, say, the first month of gestation, they would not
become persons and, therefore, they would not *be* persons during that
first month. Now, it is surely mysterious that what a fetus *is* now depends, not on traits it presently has, but on traits it will develop.

The source of this mystery is the idea that the same continuous entity
must have the same continuous essence. It is this that enables the infer-
ence from the fact that a fetus is a phase of the same continuous entity
as an adult person, to the conclusion that the fetus has the same
essence (and thus the same moral status) as the adult person—
irrespective of the fetus's actual traits. But the claim that the same continuous entity must have the same continuous essence is more complex
than meets the eye.

Everything hinges on what makes something the *same continuous entity*. If continuous possession of the same essence is what makes something the same continuous entity, then the claim that the same continuous entity must have the same continuous essence is true because it is

---

53. Lee, *Abortion and Unborn Human Life*, 5–6, 55.
54. I am indebted to Susan Dwyer for this formulation of the argument.

a tautology. Being the same continuous entity means being something with the same continuous essence (and vice versa). But, notice that this is not enough to say that a fetus has the same essence—personhood—as an adult human being. The reason is that it is (at least) equally *logically* possible to say that adults have their essential natures as persons only once they develop the traits that are normally identified with (substantive) persons—reason, self-consciousness, and so on. And the stages before that happens are stages of a *different entity*, as perhaps a caterpillar is a different entity from the butterfly that emerges from it.

If this seems implausible regarding humans, it is because we are accustomed to thinking that any physically continuous entity is the same entity over time. However, once we say that the sameness of an entity is determined by physical continuity, the link between continuous entity and continuous essence stops being tautological. The claim that, if an entity has an essential nature, then it must have that essential nature for the whole time that it is the same continuous physical entity is not a tautology. There is no logical problem with the same continuous physical entity undergoing a change from one essence to another.

Indeed, consider what happens when a human being dies. The corpse that remains is physically continuous with the living human, yet we would normally think that the corpse *was* a person, not that it still is. And that means that something can be the same continuous physical entity and undergo a change in essence. But, if it can happen at the end of life, there is no reason that it cannot happen at the beginning. Then, we could grant that the fetus is the same continuous physical entity with the child to come, who will surely be a person, but that the fetus is not a person, because a change in essence has intervened.

Suppose we insist that the same continuous physical entity must have the same essence. Then, we should say that the corpse is a person. Indeed, since Lee suggests that being a living organism (along with intelligence and freedom) is part of the essence of persons, his argument will lead us to conclude that the corpse is alive! If it seems absurd to claim that a corpse is alive though it lacks life, note that this is just the mirror image of the claim that the fetus is a (substantive) person, though it lacks such traits of (substantive) personhood as intelligence and freedom. But, of course, this is absurd, and that means that it is absurd at both ends. To be alive, you must have the traits of the living. To be a person, you must have the traits of persons. Mere physical continuity with something that will have those traits, or that did have them, will not do the job.

The seeming plausibility of the idea that the same continuous physical entity has the same continuous essence arises from conflating two different definitions of *same continuous entity*. On one definition, a thing is the same continuous entity if it has the same continuous essence; on the other definition, a thing is the same continuous entity if it is a physically continuous entity. If we stick to the first definition, the same physically continuous entity can undergo essential change and become a different entity as a result. If we stick to the second, the same physically continuous entity can undergo essential change.

Either of these alternatives undermines Lee's argument. On the first alternative, though a fetus is physically continuous with an adult person, the fetus is not ipso facto the same entity as the adult person and thus not ipso facto a person. On the second alternative, though a fetus is the same entity as an adult person, it does not thereby have the same continuous essence and thus, again, is not ipso facto a person. Notice, too, that either of these alternatives removes the mysterious claim that fetuses can be (substantive) persons though they lack the traits of (substantive) personhood.

Now, if an entity's moral status depends on its essential nature, then since physical identity does not entail essential identity, physical identity does not entail moral identity either. If, on the other hand, an entity's moral status depends on its nonessential properties, then since physical identity is compatible with changes in nonessential properties, it follows as well that physical identity does not entail moral identity. Since an entity's moral status must depend on either its essential nature or its nonessential properties (or both), it follows generally that physical identity does not imply moral identity.

Moreover, there are good reasons to believe that human beings' moral status can change profoundly with changes in their nonessential properties. For example, though innocent human beings are, for Lee, intrinsically valuable and have therefore a right to life, guilty human beings may lose their right to life (say, by justly deserving the death penalty because they have murdered, or by participating in an unjust military attack). This is not to say that such people lose their right to life entirely—the justly condemned murderer still has the right not to be killed by his fellow inmates, and the attacking soldier has the right not to be killed by his sergeant. However, each loses enough of the right to life to allow for their permissible killing, and that is what counts here. And, since neither guilt or soldierhood is an essential property of a human being, it follows that beings who have the right to life at one point can lose it (or a significant part of it) without undergoing a change in their essence—and certainly without becoming different physical beings than they were before they became guilty or drafted. But, if a being's possession of a right to life can change with the (nonessential) change from innocent to guilty or from noncombatant to soldier, then parity of reason requires that its possession of that right can change with the (nonessential) change from nonaware to self-aware. And that shows that moral identity is not implied by physical identity.

It might be objected that people who are justifiably killed because they are guilty of, say, murder do not lose their right to life, or even a part of it. Rather they retain the full right, but it is overridden due to the need to give them their just deserts. But I think that this is mistaken. If someone retains a right though we justifiably override it, we should feel regret about the fact that we have, even with good reason, trampled his right. This can surely happen. This is how we ought to think about people who, because of a (justified) program of affirmative action, have lost out on jobs for which they were qualified—or about people who have been pulled away from their normal lives because their country needed them to serve in a (justified) war. It is not how we should think about people who have rightly had their lives taken as punishment for murder. Assuming for the moment that capital punishment is just punishment for murder, we may regret having to impose it, but not because we feel we are overriding a right that the murderer retains. If I am correct here, it follows that people can lose (a significant part of) their right to life by undergoing a nonessential change. However, even if the idea that murderers' or attacking soldiers' rights are being overridden (rather than lost) is accepted, it still follows that people's *effective* moral rights can change as a result of a nonessential change. Either way, the argument from physical identity to moral identity fails. Physical identity does not imply moral identity.

It is worth noting, before moving on, that, even if Lee's argument worked and the fetus had the same essential personhood as the adult it will normally become, that would still not account for asymmetry. We would still need an argument for why it is wrong to kill persons if we replace them with others, and for why it is significantly more immoral to kill a person than not to produce a new one.

The Sacredness of Life

Sometimes what I have characterized as the asymmetric value of life is thought to be captured in saying that we view human life as sacred. In his book *Life's Dominion*, Ronald Dworkin takes this tack and goes on to argue for a legal right to abortion on the grounds that a free society ought not to legally impose some citizens' views about what is sacred upon other citizens. Such views are, Dworkin contends, essentially religious views, and imposing them on citizens would violate the U.S. Constitution's protection of the "free exercise of religion." In arguing that we regard human life as sacred, Dworkin asserts, "The hallmark of the sacred as distinct from the incrementally valuable is that the sacred is intrinsically *valuable because*—and therefore only once—*it exists*."[55] Notice that holding something valuable because, and therefore only once, it exists is tantamount to holding it to have asymmetric value (Dworkin sometimes uses the term "inviolable"), for the value lies in the existing one, which thus is not equaled in value by a possible future one that might replace it.

The problem is to explain what it is that makes human life valuable in this asymmetric way. Dworkin tries to do this by giving two examples of other things we value as sacred: works of great art and distinct animal species. What our valuation of them shares, which Dworkin calls "the nerve of the sacred," is that we value the process that has brought them into existence. Individual human life is, for Dworkin, all the more eligible for sacredness than are works of art or nature because it is, so to speak, the product of both natural processes and human creative efforts. But our valuing of the natural processes and the human creative efforts that bring something into existence does not explain (much less justify) our asymmetric valuing of that thing. If it did, then we would value asymmetrically—find sacred—*every product* of human effort or of natural processes, which we obviously do not, and surely should not. Dworkin appears to recognize this untoward result of his argument and notes that "[w]e do not treat everything that human beings create as sacred." But he offers no principle to account for our selectiveness here. Instead, he attributes it to a "complex network of feelings and intuitions," which he admits might be no more than "inconsistent superstitions."[56] Clearly, though Dworkin has noted the asymmetric value of human life, he has no good account of what it is about human life that justifies valuing it asymmetrically. Hence, he has done no more than call attention to the problem; he has no solution.

Loss of a Future Life like Ours

Don Marquis holds that "loss of a future life" is what makes killing human adults and human fetuses equally wrong: "Since the loss of the future to a standard fetus, if killed, is . . . at least as great a loss as the

---

55. Ronald Dworkin, *Life's Dominion: An Argument about Abortion, Euthanasia, and Individual Freedom* (New York: Vintage Books, 1994), 73–74 (emphasis added). Dworkin's argument that beliefs about the sacredness (or sanctity) of life are inherently religious in nature and thus that laws against abortion run afoul of the Constitution's protection of religious freedom occupies much of his chapter 6.

56. Dworkin, *Life's Dominion*, 80–81.

loss of the future to a standard adult human being who is killed, abortion . . . is presumptively very seriously wrong, where that presumption is very strong—as strong as the presumption that killing another adult human being is wrong."[57]

Consider, however, that we do not view every premature stopping of a natural process as a loss. If a rose seed is planted but not watered and thus dies, we do not say that the seed has *lost* its rose-future. More accurate would be to say that its rose-future failed to occur. On the other hand, if an adult human being is murdered, we say that he *lost* the future life he would have otherwise had. A pro-choicer thinks that an aborted fetus is like the seed and not like the murdered adult. Marquis has simply assumed the reverse. He has not provided an argument for why the fetus should count as a being that can *lose* its future, as opposed to merely as a being whose future phases may fail to occur.

Marquis appears to deal with this problem when he responds to the objection that an embryo cannot be a victim, as put forth in an article by Paul Bassen. Bassen contends that embryos cannot be victims because they lack sentience or other mental activity, and he poses the counterexample of plants, which, though living, cannot be victims.[58] Against this, Marquis argues that plants cannot be victims because "killing them cannot deprive them of a future like ours." But notice that this makes the issue of whether a being can be a victim hinge on *what* it can be deprived of, rather than on whether it can be *deprived* of anything at all. What I said about loss applies equally to deprivation. The unwatered rose seed is not deprived of its rose-future; a rose seed is not the sort of thing that can be deprived of anything. To think it is, is to impute victimizability to it and thereby to beg the question. Which is precisely what Marquis does when he says against Bassen, "Of course, embryos can be victims: when their lives are deliberately terminated, they are *deprived* of their futures of value, their prospects. This makes them victims, for it directly wrongs them."[59] This puts the cart before the horse. To assert that cutting short their lives deprives embryos of something, as opposed to merely causing some future phase not to occur, is to assume in advance that embryos can be victims of morally relevant losses. Since what the embryo is thought capable of losing in a morally relevant way is its life, this is tantamount to ascrib-

---

57. Don Marquis, "Why Abortion Is Immoral," *Journal of Philosophy* 86, no. 4 (April 1989): 183–202 (quotation from p. 194).

58. See Paul Bassen, "Present Sakes and Future Prospects: The Status of Early Abortion," *Philosophy and Public Affairs* 11, no. 4 (1982): 314–37, esp. 322–26.

59. Marquis, "Why Abortion Is Immoral," 200 (emphasis in original).

ing moral vulnerability to murder to embryos. And, since that is what is at issue in the argument about abortion, Marquis has begged the question by assuming precisely what he must prove.

The main abortion arguments do not work. In the next chapter, I shall try to draw the lessons from this failure and use them to point us toward an argument that will succeed.

3

Abortion, Infanticide, and the Ways We Value Human Life

> Why . . . has it been imagined that to die is an evil—when it is
> clear that not to have been, before our birth, was no evil?
>
> Voltaire, *A Philosophical Dictionary*

Intuitions, Infants, Intrinsic Value, and Existence

As I suggested in the introduction, the key—or rather the keyhole that shows us the shape of the key—to the moral problem of abortion lies in the fact that anyone who thinks that human beings are *morally vulnerable to murder* (at some point from conception on) values the lives of living human beings *asymmetrically*. This means that, when we hold that it is immoral to kill a human being or let one die, we are not just valuing the good traits possessed by human beings. We are valuing that those humans who are already living, go on living. This is what has to be accounted for if our beliefs about the wrongness of killing humans are to have a rational foundation.

Recall what I referred to in the introduction as the direction of my argument. I do not aim to prove that we ought to value human beings asymmetrically. Rather, I start with the existing conceptual framework used by both pro-lifers and pro-choicers. Both already think that, if it is ever gravely immoral to kill a human being, then (1) it is gravely immoral even if that human being is replaced by another one; and (2) it is far more immoral than for fertile couples not to procreate due to contraception or abstinence (if that is immoral at all). My method is to

This chapter is based upon my "Abortion, Infanticide, and the Asymmetric Value of Human Life," *Journal of Social Philosophy* 27, no. 3 (Winter 1996): 181–200; and my "Abortion, Infanticide, and the Changing Grounds of the Wrongness of Killing: Reply to Don Marquis's 'Reiman on Abortion,' " *Journal of Social Philosophy* 29, no. 2 (Fall 1998): 168–74.

look for something that can be reasonably valued in a way that implies these aspects of asymmetric value. Anyone who does not believe these things—anyone who thinks that killing one human being would be made good by replacing him with a new one, anyone who thinks that not procreating is morally equivalent to murder—is not touched by my argument. But such people clearly are not thinking about the wrongness of killing human beings in the way that people engaged in the dispute about abortion are thinking. And, I would say, they are not thinking about it in the way just about everyone who thinks it is morally murder to kill a human being thinks.

As we begin to look for the kind of property (or properties) a human must possess to be an appropriate target of asymmetric valuing, bear in mind four key lessons of the previous chapter. First, though the fetus is a human being, that fact cannot provide a rational ground for attributing vulnerability to murder to fetuses. That would amount to granting fetuses a special moral status simply because they are members of our species—a case of what I have referred to above as *species-ism*. Speciesism is inadequate because it is structurally analogous to racism or sexism; like them, it arbitrarily favors members of one's own group. To show that ascribing a special moral status to humans is not arbitrary in the way that racism or sexism is, we must say what it is about human beings that makes it reasonable to grant them special status while it is not reasonable to grant special status to Caucasians or men simply because they are white or male. This will require identifying some property of humans that justifies the attribution to them of moral vulnerability to murder. We must identify this property, not the species membership—or kind—of the being who possesses the property.

We seek a property, not a kind. Even if the property were strictly coterminous with the kind (for example, a human genetic code in the case of humans), it will be the property that does the moral work, not the kind. On the other hand, once it is clear that it is a property we seek, we cannot take it for granted that the property is coterminous with the kind. We look for a property (ever) possessed by human beings that explains the asymmetric immorality of killing them—all the while leaving open whether the property is possessed by all human beings or at all stages. To answer the abortion question, we must determine whether that property is possessed by fetuses.

Second, we cannot assume dogmatically that infants are morally vulnerable to murder. I shall argue that infants do have a moral status that makes it immoral to kill them or let them die, but this will be the conclusion of an argument, not a starting point. No doubt, most of us have strong intuitions about the wrongness of killing infants. While we must use our intuitions to guide our moral reflections, we must also bear in mind that they are fallible. We may use them as clues or hypotheses, but not as moral facts or axioms. Overreliance on our intuitions is especially dangerous in the case of those about infants, since, as I shall point out later, there are biological grounds for our strong natural feelings toward infants and these feelings might easily be misidentified as intuitions about infants' moral standing. Further, assuming infants' rights in advance overlooks the reasoned arguments (by Warren, Tooley, Benn, and others) that cast doubt on the idea that infants have the same kind of moral standing that children and adults do.

Third, that we seek a property, not a kind, complements the notion that physical identity does not imply moral identity. This is because a property may come to be possessed by a being only at some point during its existence, while the being remains the same physical thing throughout its existence. Nonetheless, we have seen Lee argue that, if a property bestows moral status, then a being that has that property at some point in its physical existence has that moral status for the whole duration of its physical existence. I have shown that this argument is based on confounding two different notions of what it means to be the same continuous thing and that the argument results in the mystery that a newly conceived zygote is a person even though it lack the traits of personhood (rational thinking, self-consciousness, and so on). Moreover, I have shown that moral rights change profoundly, or at least that *effective* moral rights change profoundly, with nonessential changes in a being, such as going from innocent to guilty, or from noncombatant to soldier. This conclusion adds a new dimension to the idea that it is a property, not a kind, that we seek. Moral rights will belong to a being not simply because it possesses the relevant property at some time in its career, *but only once it has that property.*

Fourth, the property must account for asymmetry. Writers like Lee, who assert that human beings have intrinsic value, or like Dworkin, who hold that life is sacred, are clearly aware that human life has value of a special sort, that is, asymmetric value. But saying "intrinsic value" explains neither how or why intrinsic value implies asymmetry nor what it is about human beings that gives them intrinsic value. Much the same can be said of the "sacredness" or "sanctity" of life and of "human beings as ends-in-themselves." All of these phrases evoke asymmetry but give no rational account of it. Unless we can identify something about human beings that accounts for asymmetry, these incantations are no more than acts of faith. They express the hope for an explanation of what it is about humans that makes it wrong to kill them even if one replaces them, and worse to kill them than not to produce new ones. They are not, however, the explanations themselves.

The asymmetry in asymmetric value is that the value lost in destroying an existing human being is significantly greater than the value that can be gained by adding a new human being. It might seem that there are easy ways of explaining this asymmetry. For example, destroying an existent thing wastes the effort that already went into producing it, while not producing it does not. Likewise, trying to produce a new one courts a risk of failure, while an existing one is a sure thing. Thus, considerations of wasted effort, uncertainty, and the like make it worse to destroy an existing thing than not to produce a new one. However, these considerations are not large enough to account for the very large moral difference that people generally think exists between killing an existing human being and not bringing a new one into existence. Those who think that killing an existing human is gravely immoral even if the killer replaces the killed one with a new live one would not change their minds if the killer took on the costs and risks of producing the new one, or even if the killer compensated for the costs and risks of producing the killed one.[1] Consequently, the costs and risks of producing a new human being cannot account for the asymmetric value of existing human beings.

Nor, by the way, can we explain why murder is worse than not procreating by recourse to the so-called acts-omissions principle, which holds that acting to produce a bad outcome is always much worse than simply failing to prevent that same outcome. This principle is far from universally accepted, so we cannot assume that it holds in the controversial cases we are here considering. Anyway, contraception and abstinence are acts, so they get no special dispensation from the principle. Consequently, if murder is worse than refraining from procreating, it is not because the former is an act and the latter an omission.

Since asymmetric valuing of human life places special value on the particular living individual, it might seem that we could asymmetri-

---

1. If the moral difference between killing and not procreating were due to the loss of investment that results from killing, then this would surely not be a large enough difference to make abortions as bad as killing children or adults, since abortions come when there is much less investment than goes into raising babies to become children and children to become adults. Similar things can be said about risk. The probability of producing a fetus that reaches the stage at which most abortions occur is much greater than the probability of producing an offspring that survives until childhood or adulthood. Consequently, abortions occur when the risk of failure involved in trying to reproduce is smaller than the risk of failing to have offspring that reach childhood. In any event, until birth, both the investment and the risk are the pregnant woman's and thus hers to waste or venture.

cally value a particular embryo. Insofar as each embryo is a distinct particular with its own genetic code, this line of thought runs, we could value the particular embryo itself and then regard its ending as a loss of a particular that cannot be made good by replacing it with a new one, since the new embryo would be a different one with a different genetic code. This implies, to be sure, that it is logically possible to value asymmetrically the particular embryo a pregnant woman is carrying. However, there is no reasonable ground for valuing that particular embryo asymmetrically. This is because, until the embryo develops recognizable distinctive traits, its particularity is purely negative. We simply know that it has a distinct genetic code that is different from other ones. We do not know the positive content of this difference. And, without that positive content, there is no reason to prefer this particular one over a new one, which would be particular in just the same way. Another way to see this is that, in losing the particular embryo currently in a pregnant woman, no more is lost than was lost when that woman did not conceive at another time.[2] That, too, would have been a particular embryo with its own genetic code. In short, the particularity of a given embryo is enough to make it the object of asymmetric valuation, but not enough to account for the reasonableness of such valuation, since there is no reason to prefer one particular embryo over another particular one.

Nor, of course, as I observed in the introduction, can one account for the asymmetric value of human life by holding, with the deontologist, that killing a human is worse than refusing to procreate because killing is a greater violation of duty, or with the virtue-ethicist, that killing is worse because it manifests a more evil character. For killing a human is a greater violation of duty or manifests a worse character than refusing to procreate only if it is worse to kill a human being than to refuse to create one, even though both acts result in there being one less human being. Thus both the deontologist's and the virtue-ethicist's claim presuppose the asymmetric value of human life rather than provide an explanation of it.

One may be tempted to say that the explanation of the asymmetry between the loss from murder and the gain from procreating is provided by the value of *existence* itself. That would provide just the difference between killing an existing human being and not creating one. However, rejection of the idea that physical identity implies moral

---

2. It is, I hope, clear that I am speaking of loss here only with respect to what the embyro itself amounts to. To be sure, a woman who loses her embryo in mid-pregnancy may undergo a deeply painful experience of loss that is morally relevant—but not to the value of the particular embryo as such.

identity implies that existence as such does not make a moral differ-ence. To paraphrase Kant, existence is not a morally relevant property.[3]

Consider the following. It may turn out that the fetus possesses, from the moment of conception, the property that makes killing it seri-ously wrong. Then, its physical and moral identity in this regard will coincide. However, given the possibility that this property is acquired later (either during pregnancy or later still), the fetus may exist for some time without the property. Since the fetus's physical identity with the human being that will have the property does not entail their moral identity, it follows that the pre-property fetus has no moral claim to the property, or to the moral status it carries. Moreover, since what that status gives is precisely the moral wrongness of killing the fetus, there is nothing morally wrong with ending the fetus's life be-fore the property is there. The fetus's existence prior to its possession of the property gives it no moral claim to continue existing. Thus there is no moral difference between a fetus whose existence is ended before it gets the property and a fetus that never starts to exist.

If this seems counterintuitive, I think it is because we tend to read a kind of personal identity backwards into fetuses, and personal identity carries connotations of moral identity beyond mere physical identity. If we think of the pre-property fetus as a kind of quasi-person "who" loses the chance to have the special property, then we will think of the pre-property fetus as a personlike victim—which is a moral status that a not-yet-existing fetus lacks. Just because it is so natural to us to think this way, I believe that this "retroactive empersonment" is the single greatest source of confusion in the abortion debate. (Marquis's promis-ing argument, considered at the close of chapter 2, was a case of retro-active empersonment.) If we resist retroactive empersonment, then the fact that the pre-property fetus has already been existing has no bear-ing on the moral status of its loss of future existence. Consequently, that loss is morally equivalent to the simple failure of that future stretch of fetal life to begin.

It is, however, no easy matter to account for reasonable asymmetric valuing. To start that discussion, let us consider the different sorts of value that entities might have and some different ways in which we might value entities.

Values, Objective and Subjective

None of the traits normally thought to justify imputing objective value to human life—rationality, creativity, capacity for loving attachment,

---

3. " '*Being*' is obviously not a real predicate; that is, it is not a concept of something which could be added to the concept of a thing" (Immanuel Kant, *Critique of Pure Reason*, trans. Norman Kemp Smith [London: Macmillan, 1963], 504 [emphasis in original]).

and the like—will account for the way in which we think murder is immoral. Any of these traits is as much a reason for creating new humans as for not destroying existing ones. Thus to value human beings because of these traits would lead to the outcome that creating a new human would bring into existence just as much value as killing a previous one took away. And that implies both that replacing a killed person leaves the world with no net moral loss from her killing and that it would be about equally wrong not to procreate as to commit murder.

By an *objective value*, I mean a value that is real whether or not anyone experiences it as such. What I call *objective values*, others have called *intrinsic values*. However, intrinsic value is defined by opposition to instrumental value, so that things with intrinsic value are thought to be valuable even if they serve no further goal. Objective value, by contrast, is defined by opposition to subjective value. An objective value is one that is valuable whether or not anyone is aware of it, whereas a subjective value is a value to an aware subject. The goodness of the feeling of pleasure and the goodness of food to the hungry are subjective values. (This is not to deny that both pleasure and food, not to mention the working of food on a hungry digestive system, are objective events in the world, and that they may also do objective good.) It is the opposition between objective and subjective values, rather than that between intrinsic and instrumental values, that is pertinent to the present discussion.

An entity or a property that has objective value makes the world a better place (whether or not anyone experiences it as such). That an entity has objective value, however, is roughly as good a reason for creating new ones as for not destroying old ones. By this I am not merely referring to a conventional feature of our valuing. Rather, I have in mind something about the nature of values themselves, namely, that they tend to exert their "pull" on our rational judgments and actions in all temporal dimensions. The objective value of, say, a body of knowledge or a thing of beauty really is—not just is conventionally thought to be—roughly an equal reason for preserving existing knowledge or beautiful things and for finding new knowledge or creating new beautiful things. It follows that the objective value of human beings cannot account for their asymmetric value. Objective value cannot be the object of asymmetric valuing.

I contend that the object of the asymmetric valuing of human life is the subjective value that that ongoing life has to the one whose life it is. For life to have this sort of subjective value, the one whose life it is must be aware that he is alive and, at a minimum, care about or count upon staying alive. It should be obvious that, for each individual who consciously cares about his life continuing, that continuing has asymmetric value. Such an individual values his own continuing far more

highly than he values his own death followed by replacement by another living individual. And such an individual normally thinks that
his dying is worse than his not having been born—as Voltaire's question, quoted at the outset of this chapter, reminds us.

But note that this is not enough. This much gives us the asymmetric
value of a human life *to the individual whose life it is*. It does not give us
the asymmetric *moral* value of human life. A *moral* value is one that all
people should recognize. Thus the moral value of life—while it may be
based on the value a life has to the one whose life it is—must be the
value of each individual's life as recognized by every other (moral)
individual. Thus, to account for the asymmetric moral value of human
life, we need to consider how people generally might value that beings
who consciously care about the continuation of their lives get to go on
living.

To see how this comes into the picture, let us now consider the ways
in which people value things.

Ways of Valuing

In focusing on valuing, I do not mean to suggest that things get their
value from our valuing them or that things will have whatever value
we attach to them. Quite the contrary, my argument is that our valu-
ings have rational basis only if their objects have features that make the
way we value them appropriate. So far, I have suggested that what we
are valuing when we value human life asymmetrically is the individual's own subjective valuation of his life. Now we need to consider the
ways in which we can value things, to see how we can value individuals' own subjective valuation of their lives asymmetrically, that is, in a
way that does not imply that existing and future lives are of roughly
equal value.

Categorical, Individual, and Conditional Valuing

Consider the difference between (1) my valuing Ws, (2) my valuing
this particular X, and (3) my valuing that Ys who want Z get Z. In (1),
my valuing implies that I think that existing Ws should be preserved
and that more Ws should be brought into existence, if possible. To see
this, substitute for W "creative human beings." My valuing of such
beings implies that creative humans should not be stopped from being
creative but also that it would be good to bring more creative human
beings into existence. In (2), my valuing implies that the particular X
that I value should continue in existence, but it does not imply that it

would be good to bring some new X into existence, since that would be a different one from the particular one that I value. This will be clear if we substitute for X "friend." My valuing of a particular friend implies valuing that she continue to exist but not that any new friend be brought into existence. My valuing in (3) implies that I think that Ys should get what they want, but it does not imply that Ys who want Z should be brought into existence so that they can get Z. Substitute for Y "starving human beings," and for Z "food." Then it is clear that my valuing of starving human beings getting the food they want implies that starving human beings should be allowed to eat and perhaps be provided with food if they cannot fend for themselves—but it surely does not imply that more starving human beings should be brought into existence so that they can get the food they want.

I call valuing of the first sort *categorical*, valuing of the second sort *individual*, and valuing of the third sort *conditional*. The latter is conditional in that my valuing of Ys getting Z can be stated as the following conditional: *If and only if* there exist Ys wanting Z, then I value their getting Z. Individual valuing is also conditional in that I can value a particular individual *if and only if* she already exists.

No *categorical* valuing of human life will account for asymmetry. This is because such valuing values roughly equally preserving existing valued ones and creating new ones. Then, destroying one valued entity and replacing it with another will lead to no net loss in valued entities. (As we saw in the introduction, even great paintings, such as Van Gogh's *Wheat Field with Crows*, can be replaced by identical duplicates without loss.) And destroying one valued entity will cost the world about as much value as refraining from creating a new one. Note that I am not denying that we do value human life categorically. We do and we should. Categorical valuing of human life leads us to want to continue the existence of the human race, to promote and perhaps provide for the existence of some optimal number of living human beings, and so on. However, categorical valuing of human life will not account for the wrongness of murder, because the human race can remain in existence or even exist in some optimal number, though some are killed and replaced by others.

On the other hand, both the individual or the conditional valuing of human life are forms of asymmetric valuing. By *individual* valuing of human life, I mean the way I value either my own life or the life of some other particular human being. This implies valuing that a particular existing human stay alive, but it does not imply valuing that any new human be brought into existence. By *conditional* valuing of human life, I mean valuing that human beings who want to live get to do so. This implies valuing that existing humans who want to stay alive do.

But it does not imply valuing that new humans who will want to stay alive be created so that they can get what they want, because it implies nothing about whether it is better to want and get to live than not to have lived at all. Consequently, neither individual nor conditional valuing of human life will imply that killing one human and replacing him with a living one yields no net loss in value. Nor does either imply that killing one human and failing to replace him are roughly equally bad.

Wanting, Loving, Respecting

Though I shall use these terms with sharper boundaries than they have in ordinary talk, I think it is fair to say that *wanting* is categorical valuing, *loving* is individual valuing, *respecting* is conditional valuing. When we want something, like ice cream or a motorcycle, we want that type of thing and not any particular instance of it. We may, of course, want Breyer's chocolate-chip ice cream or a particular model of Harley-Davidson motorcycle, but still any box of Breyer's chocolate-chip ice cream or any Harley in that particular model will do. Wanting human beings to live does not amount to valuing their lives asymmetrically, since, as categorical valuing, such wanting is satisfied with there being some substantial number of living humans, with no particular preference for one individual over another. Though I shall have more to say about wanting later, loving and respecting are for the moment more promising bases for asymmetric value. Let us, then, consider the ways in which the *lover* and the *respecter* each value their objects.

Love, though it may be triggered by the appeal of certain traits or properties of the beloved, is a way of valuing the beloved as such—"unconditionally," we sometimes say—and thus of valuing the sheer existence of the beloved. I include here our natural love of our fellows, the sentiment that Hume called "humanity."[4] It is a cherishing of our fellows' sheer existence. Since love of an individual or of our fellows goes beyond the traits that trigger it to cherish the sheer existence of its object, love cannot be based ultimately on any feature of its object. Any feature could be replaced by finding another individual with it, and therefore no feature can account for love's valuing of the sheer existence of the beloved.

Respect, though it is aimed at individuals, is a way of valuing their capacity to place value on things. In the words of Kant quoted earlier, "When I observe the duty of respect, I . . . keep myself within my own

---

4. David Hume, *An Enquiry Concerning the Principles of Morals* (Indianapolis, IN: Hackett, 1983; originally published 1751), 75.

bounds in order not to deprive another of any of the value which he as a human being is entitled to put upon himself."[5] Respect is conditional valuing because it values that the respected one get what he or she values (subject, of course, to being limited or overridden when the thing valued conflicts with things of comparable or greater value to others, and to being defeated if the thing valued is evil), and thus respect is conditional upon the respected one existing and valuing something.

In contrast to love, respect is due to something about the respected one that leads us to care about her getting what she wants. In this sense, respect is *deserved* by the respected because of what leads us to value her getting what she values. By contrast, love is *given* freely by the lover. Love expresses the attitude—what a poet might call the "passion"—of the lover, while respect responds to something thought worthy in the respected.

Moreover, while the lover values the existence of the beloved, the respecter values that the respected gets what she values. Consequently, the loss of the loved object is a loss to the lover, but the failure of the respected to get what she values is a loss to the respected. This is important because it implies that respect is a stronger basis for ascribing a moral right to protection of its object's life than love is. The loss of life to the respected one is a total and unredeemable loss. The loss of the loved one is a loss to the lover but not a loss of the lover's very existence. The lover lives on to love again.

Respect as Reasonable Asymmetrical Valuing

Love expresses the disposition of the lover; it does not respond to something independently worthy in the beloved. Love cherishes the particular behind the traits, not the traits themselves—if it cherished the traits, it would be content with another particular with those traits. Love, then, strictly speaking, loves the particular for no good reason rooted in the particular's nature. Thus, while love makes the beloved asymmetrically valuable *to the lover*, it does not imply that the beloved is asymmetrically valuable *itself*. Respect, by contrast, implies that there is something asymmetrically valuable in the object of respect it-

---

5. Immanuel Kant, "The Metaphysical Principles of Virtue," pt. 2 of *The Metaphysics of Morals*, in *Ethical Philosophy*, trans. James W. Ellington (Indianapolis, IN: Hackett, 1983; originally published 1797), 114; see also Kant's *Groundwork of the Metaphysics of Morals*, trans. James W. Ellington (Indianapolis, IN: Hackett, 1981; originally published 1785), 35–37. While I think my account of respect is in line with Kant's, I do not put it forth as a gloss on Kant's.

self. In this section, I will show that there is good reason to respect human beings' conscious caring about their lives. Consequently, there is good reason to believe in the asymmetric value of consciously cared about lives.

We have good reason to respect people's subjective valuation of their lives because, once conscious caring has come on the scene, the ending of a life that is cared about causes a loss to the one whose life it is that cannot be made good by replacing that life with another living individual. Consequently, there is good reason for believing in the greater wrongness of ending a consciously cared about life than of not creating a new one, and thus good reason for believing in the asymmetric value of such human life.

When I say that the ending of a life that is consciously cared about causes a loss, I am not speaking of the loss felt by one who knows he is about to die. The wrong involved in being killed is the loss of the life of which one has begun to be aware; it is not the pain of being aware of losing one's life. Causing the latter pain is a wrong to be sure, one that may make it worse to kill someone who is aware of what's happening than, say, to kill him in his sleep. But killing someone in his sleep is bad enough to count as murder, and that is what counts here. Consequently, I am not arguing that ending the life of a human being who is aware of and caring about his life is wrong because it thwarts a felt desire to stay alive or a conscious belief that one will. Rather, our inquiry has led us to a unique human vulnerability and to a distinctive moral response to that vulnerability. Once a human being has begun to be aware of his life, that life unfolds before a kind of inner audience—the self—that has an expectation of its continuation, an affective stake in living on. This expectation persists until the audience shuts down for good—even if, before that, the audience dozes off from time to time. In other words, this expectation does not only characterize the individual while he is aware of it. It becomes part of his self. Consequently, we defeat this expectation even if we kill a temporarily sleeping or comatose individual who has begun to be aware of his life.

Suppose I desire and expect to fly to Paris and, while I am asleep, someone steals my ticket (the last available one) for his own use. Surely the thief has frustrated my desire, thwarted my expectation, even though I am sleeping and not currently consciously desiring or expecting to fly to Paris. The point is that desires and expectations become mine once they get going, and don't stop being mine just because I am not thinking about them. And indeed, when I wake up and think again about my desire, I do not experience this as a new (case of) desire to fly to Paris. Rather, I experience myself as revisiting my earlier desire and continuing it, so to speak, seamlessly. My period of being asleep, rather than feeling like a break in my desires and expectations, feels like an occurrence within my history as a being with these desires and expectations. This is what I mean by speaking of my life as occurring before an inner audience.

There might seem to be a kind of sleight of hand here. After all, my consciousness does shut down while I am in dreamless sleep or a temporary coma. So it seems that I must be deluded in thinking that my sleep or coma happens within the history of my consciousness, before my inner audience. But this is an illusion only if one insists that the audience must always be attentive to be an audience. To be sure, the self is not some metaphysical substance abiding through sleep and wakefulness. Since Hume, we have recognized that there is no "I" in the sense of a substance, or something that we can grasp or picture. But this only means that the self is not a thing but a kind of functional reality. I experience it as the space from which my actions seem to emanate, to which my memories attach, and around which my motives, hopes, desires, and expectations gather.

The human self is the audience that comes into existence with the dawn of self-awareness and persists until self-awareness shuts down for good (in death or permanent unconsciousness). This self is not an enduring substance. It is more like an inner holograph projected backwards from the actions, memories, motives, hopes, desires, and expectations that cluster around it and give it, so to speak, its shape. Though not a substance, it is my "point of view," the real place where "I" live and from which I experience my life as mine—from which I even experience my dreamless sleep as *my* rest. I contend that it is this self that is aware of and cares about the continuation of my life and that the asymmetric protection of my life is a way of protecting the desires and expectations of this self. Because of the special kind of inner awareness that constitutes the self, humans are vulnerable to a special loss from the ending of a life already underway. *Our moral beliefs about the wrongness of murder make sense only as, in effect, a collective undertaking by human beings to protect one another against this loss.*

It isn't easy to capture the way in which staying alive becomes specially important to us once we are aware of it, though I think everyone can recognize it in his or her own experience. One writer who has given expression to something of what is at stake here is Richard Wollheim. Death, Wollheim argues, is a misfortune even when life is bad:

> It is not that death deprives us of some particular pleasure, or even of pleasure. What it deprives us of is something more fundamental than pleasure: it deprives us of that thing which we gain access to when, as persisting creatures, we enter into our present mental states. . . . It de-

prives us of phenomenology [subjective awareness itself], and, having once tasted phenomenology, we develop a longing for it which we cannot give up: not even when the desire for cessation of pain, for extinction, grows stronger.[6]

And Aristotle observed in the *Politics*, "that men cling to life even at the cost of enduring great misfortune, seeming to find in life a natural sweetness and happiness."[7]

The loss to an aware individual of the life whose continuation she is counting on is a loss that can exist only once an aware individual exists. Moreover, it is a loss that remains a loss, a frustration of that individual's expectations, even if that individual is replaced by another equally aware one. Thus it is a loss that can explain why ending a human life is significantly worse than not creating one. Moreover, it explains as well why the killing of an existing human being aware of her life is not made good by replacing her with a new one who will be aware. Though the result of this replacement will be no net loss in the objective value added to the world by the existence of humans, the aware individual will suffer an unredeemable disappointment of her expectations, which makes her ending a loss that cannot be made up for by creating another.

If it be thought that care about one's life is too thin a reed upon which to rest respect, remember that this care is the affective response to awareness of oneself as a being living out a life, so to speak, a minute or a day at a time—and that such awareness is available only to rational beings. This awareness is available only to rational beings because it implies recognition of one's remembered past and of one's anticipated future as phases of the same self that one is now, and as merely remembered and anticipated rather than as actually happening. This in turns seems to require some understanding of the difference between current experience and actual event, and some ability to refer to oneself and, so to speak, to date one's experiences. These competencies are only to be found in beings that we would count as rational. Consequently, to respect beings because they care about the continuation of their lives is to respect them for being rational.

It might seem that my emphasis on caring presupposes a hedonistic or subjectivist ethical framework in which *that* people want something is more important than the goodness or badness of *what* they want. But the claim I am making is more general than this, since any plausible

---

6. Richard Wollheim, *The Thread of Life* (Cambridge, MA: Harvard University Press, 1984), 269.

7. Aristotle, *Politics* 3.6.1278b, in *The Complete Works of Aristotle*, ed. Jonathan Barnes (Princeton, NJ: Princeton University Press, 1984), vol. 2, p. 2029.

morality will give some moral weight to the fact of human caring, as long as the object of that caring is either good or neutral. For example, in just about any moral theory, people's strong desire not to be in pain is reason enough to think it prima facie immoral to impose pain on people. Therefore, since the object of people's caring about the continuation of their lives going on is at least neutral and very probably good, that caring has moral weight.

For all these reasons, conscious caring about one's own life is an appropriate object of our respect, and thus accounts for the asymmetric value of human life once conscious caring is on the scene.

The Morality of Abortion

Since fetuses are not conscious that they are alive, they do not qualify for possession of asymmetric value. The result is that abortion is no worse morally than contraception or abstinence, which is to say, not immoral at all.

Let us sum up the steps in the argument that has led to this conclusion:

1. To qualify for the moral status of vulnerability to murder, a being must be a reasonable object of asymmetric valuing.
2. Objectively good traits of living beings cannot be the object of asymmetric valuing.
3. Subjective valuing of life can be the object of asymmetric valuing.
4. There is a recognizable mode of valuing subjective valuing, namely, respect.
5. There is good reason to value the subjective valuing of life, since a being who consciously cares about his or her life is subject to a special and unredeemable loss.
6. It is reasonable to respect and thus to ascribe asymmetric value to beings who consciously care about their lives.
7. Our moral beliefs about the wrongness of murder make sense only as, in effect, a collective undertaking by human beings to protect one another against the loss of the lives they consciously care about.
8. Fetuses are not conscious that they are alive.
9. The only aspect of fetuses that is a possible object of asymmetric valuing is their unique genetic code, but this is not a reasonable object of asymmetric valuing.

10. Fetuses lack any property that would make them reasonable objects of asymmetric valuing.
11. The existence of a pre-property fetus gives it no moral standing. Its death is no different than the failure of any future life to come into existence.
12. Abortion is no different morally from contraception and abstinence.
13. Abortion does not qualify morally as murder, as this concept is used by pro-lifers and pro-choicers alike.
14. Since contraception and abstinence are normally thought not to be immoral at all, abortion is likewise not immoral at all.

Persons and Ends-in-Themselves

We have seen that it is common to think that human beings have special moral rights either because they are *persons* or because they are *ends-in-themselves*. I have, however, noted that there is a striking absence of satisfactory accounts of what property qualifies human beings for these statuses and of how having that property makes it appropriate to grant humans special moral rights. So, while Mary Anne Warren gives a list of the properties conventionally associated with personhood (consciousness, reasoning, self-motivated activity, and so on), she fails to explain why any or all of these elements make it appropriate to hold a being that possesses the elements to be asymmetrically valuable.[8] After all, these properties will be replicated in any human being that comes of age, and thus it seems that one human with these properties can be killed and replaced by another, with no loss in value. Likewise, Kant holds that ends-in-themselves cannot be substituted for, but provides neither a clear idea of what about humans makes them ends-in-themselves nor why being an end-in-itself implies nonsubstitutability. Here, too, it seems, on the contrary, that one end-in-itself is as good as another and so substitutable for the other without net loss. In this section, I shall suggest what it is about persons and ends-in-themselves that makes it appropriate to value them asymmetrically.

Take personhood first. I have argued that the only reasonable basis for asymmetrically valuing human life is that humans are aware of, and counting on, the continuation of the particular lives they already have. This is possible only for a being who is aware of his self as the

---

8. Mary Anne Warren, "On the Moral and Legal Status of Abortion," in *The Problem of Abortion*, ed. Joel Feinberg, 2nd ed. (Belmont, CA: Wadsworth, 1984), 110–14.

same self enduring over time. A hallowed philosophical tradition defines personhood by this very awareness. Locke defined a *person* as "a thinking intelligent being, that . . . can consider itself as itself . . . in different times and places."[9] Kant wrote, "That which is conscious of the numerical identity of itself at different times is in so far a *person*."[10]

Not only does this argument rescue the idea that it is persons who are morally entitled to protection against killing; it also reinforces my claim that the asymmetric value of human life is based on our respect for our fellows as beings who care about their lives. Persons are commonly thought to be proper objects of respect.

Consider now ends-in-themselves. Two features characterize ends-in-themselves. First, they have value that does not depend on their being means to some value beyond them. Second, they are the sources of the value of things that are valued only as a means to something beyond them. That is, as I seek some end, say, my paycheck, I do so for some end to which it is a means, say, shelter. If shelter is yet a means to something else, say, comfort, it is not an end-in-itself. However, as Aristotle long ago pointed out, unless I have some end that I desire for its own sake and not as a means to something beyond it, my striving will be futile and pointless, since nothing will really have value for me.[11] Each goal will be valued as a means to another, which is valued as a means to another, and so on, without ever arriving at something capable of sending value back down the line to the things that are means to it. On the other hand, if I have some end that I value for its own sake, say, comfort again, then it is an end-in-itself. Its value does not depend on its being a means to something else. This end-in-itself will give value to all the means that were sought to get to it. In short, ends-in-themselves are the unmoved movers of the valuable. This suggests that we should think of ends-in-themselves less as things of very great value than as *sources of value*.[12]

Recall that, when we respect human beings, that which is the object of our respect is precisely their capacity to set values for themselves.

9. John Locke, *An Essay concerning Human Understanding*, ed. and abridged by John Yolton (London: Everyman, 1994; originally published 1690), bk. 2, chap. 27, sec. 9, 180.

10. Kant, *Critique of Pure Reason*, 341 (emphasis in original).

11. Aristotle, *Nicomachean Ethics* 1.2.1094a, in *Complete Works of Aristotle*, ed. Barnes, vol. 2, p. 1729.

12. Allan Wood has proposed an interpretation of Kant's notion of rational agents as ends-in-themselves based on the idea that ends-in-themselves are sources of value: "Rational volition is what makes it the case that other things are good. . . ." See Allan Wood, "Humanity as As End in Itself," in *Kant's Groundwork of the Metaphysics of Morals: Critical Essays*, ed. Paul Guyer (Lanham, MD: Rowman & Littlefield, 1998), 165–87 (quotation from p. 176).

If, then, we take being an end-in-itself as being capable of bestowing value on things, we have the trait of human beings that is the object of respect. Since that respect amounts to valuing that such beings get what they value, respecting ends-in-themselves will lead to protecting the things they value, such as their ongoing life.

What links ends-in-themselves to personhood is that being a source of values and being able to recognize oneself as the same particular at different points in time are features of rational beings. This, then, is what we ultimately respect when we treat human beings as asymmetrically valuable. Kant tied it all together: "Rational beings are called 'persons' inasmuch as their nature already marks them out as ends-in-themselves . . . , which are thus objects of respect."[13]

Love, Infanticide, and Fetuses

The newborn infant's level of awareness is more like a fetus's than like an adult's or a child's. It does not yet have awareness that it is alive, much less that it is the selfsame person enduring over time.[14] If being aware of one's life is the necessary condition of the objection to killing human beings, what follows about the moral status of infanticide? This question is important because some philosophers (and many nonphilosophers) take their intuition that infanticide is as wrong as killing adults or children so seriously as to rule out any account of the wrongness of killing that doesn't apply equally to infants.[15]

---

13. Kant, *Groundwork of the Metaphysics of Morals*, 36.
14. According to one expert on infant cognitive development:

[I]t is a most un-Proustian life, not thought, only lived. Sensorimotor schemata . . . enable a child to walk a straight line but not to think about a line in its absence, to recognize his or her mother but not to think about her when she is gone. It is a world difficult for us to conceive, accustomed as we are to spend much of our time ruminating about the past and anticipating the future. Nevertheless, this is the state that Piaget posits for the child before one-and-a-half, that is, an ability to recognize objects and events but an inability to recall them in their absence. Because of this inability . . . the child cannot even remember what he or she did a few minutes ago. . . . These observations have been made by others as well, but more recently there have been occasional suggestions that recall may occur considerably earlier than Piaget believed, perhaps in the second 6 months of life.

Jean M. Mandler, "Representation and Recall in Infancy," in *Infant Memory: Its Relation to Normal and Pathological Memory in Humans and Other Animals*, ed. Morris Moscovitch (New York: Plenum Press, 1984), 75–76.
15. See, for example, Michael Lockwood, "Warnock versus Powell (and Har-

The attitude that we have when we think it wrong to kill children or adults because they care about their lives going on is a form of respect. We respect their property of being aware of, and caring about, their lives (and all this brings in its wake), and we respect them for having this attribute. We show this respect by protecting their ability to get what they care about. We are not (necessarily) either caring about them independently of what they care about or directly caring about what they care about, either of which would characterize love, rather than respect.[16]

The normal reaction to infants is a loving one (though, of course, it is not the only reaction, or the only normal one). This has surely been built into us as a result of evolution. Human babies are born at a very early stage of their development and must therefore be tended to by their parents (primarily their mothers, at least until recently) for a long time before they can get along on their own, and surely for a long time before they can begin to pay their own way.[17] There are numerous evolutionary advantages of the long extrauterine development of humans. Most importantly, this long development allows adult human beings to have larger brains than could pass through a human female's birth canal. It is inconceivable that adults would have provided the necessary care for their helpless offspring over the hundreds of thousands of years of human evolution if they had not developed a strong tendency to love infants. This is love, rather than respect, precisely because it must happen automatically, before the infant can do anything to deserve or be worthy of it.

Moreover, since we are all products of this evolutionary development, the tendency to love infants is not limited to their parents or relatives. It is a general tendency in all adults, as can be testified to by the virtually universal human vulnerability to tears and to cuteness.

---

radine): When Does Potentiality Count?" *Bioethics* 2, no. 3 (1988): 187–213; Richard Werner, "Abortion: The Moral Status of the Unborn," *Social Theory and Practice* 3, no. 2 (Fall 1974): 201–22; John T. Noonan, Jr., "An Almost Absolute Value in History," in *The Problem of Abortion*, ed. Feinberg, 2nd ed., 9–14; Philip E. Devine, "The Scope of the Prohibition against Killing," in *The Problem of Abortion*, ed. Feinberg, 2nd ed., 21–42; see also Loren E. Lomasky, "Being a Person: Does It Matter?" in *The Problem of Abortion*, ed. Feinberg, 2nd ed., 161–72.

16. Of course, we will normally care in these ways too. The point is that our doing so is not necessary to the way we value the lives of children or adults. For that, all that is necessary is that we respect their caring about their lives.

17. "Human babies are the most helpless in the animal kingdom; they require many years of care before they can survive on their own" (Mary Batten, *Sexual Strategies: How Females Choose Their Mates* [New York: G.P. Putnam's Sons, 1992], 142).

Thus, the love of which I am talking is virtually a universal human phenomenon. Human beings generally love infants, not just their own. This love is directed at infants generally, even neglected or abandoned ones. Because this love is natural, virtually universally felt, and felt for all infants, I liken it to the sentiment that Hume called that of "humanity," by which he meant a natural, universal, and generalized affection for our conspecifics.[18]

Not only is this love natural and virtually universal; it is good. Some of the infants will become children and adults, and loving them as infants is a condition of their future psychological well-being. Stanley Benn acknowledges our "instinctual tenderness and protectiveness toward babies," but contends that "there is a better reason . . . for not treating infants as expendable; namely, that some infants grow up into persons. And if as infants *they* are not treated with at least some minimal degree of tenderness and consideration, they will suffer for it later, as persons."[19]

Moreover, the love that we naturally direct toward infants is arguably a necessary condition of their development into beings worthy of respect. In any event, it contributes importantly to that development. This is so for at least two reasons, and probably more. First, by loving infants, we are moved to devote the energy and attention necessary to bring them into the community of language users, which, in turn, brings them to awareness of their lives, which is a necessary condition of their caring about their lives and our respecting them for that.[20] (The *Oxford English Dictionary* gives the root of *infant* as *infans*, Latin for "unable to speak.") Second, by loving infants, we convey to them a positive valuation of their sheer existence, which, in turn, underlies and reinforces their valuation of their own particular lives once they are capable of it. Because people's own valuation of their lives is the

---

18. See note 4, above.

19. Stanley I. Benn, "Abortion, Infanticide, and Respect for Persons," in *The Problem of Abortion*, ed. Feinberg, 2nd ed., 143.

20. "When infants become *attached* to their mothers many language-critical processes are encouraged: the desire to engage in playful vocalization, including vocal exploration, the emergence of turn taking and dialogue structure, and the desire to imitate vocal patterns. In turn, mothers who are attached to and feeling nurturant toward their infants provide them with a number of opportunities to learn. Among the other processes encouraged by attachment are the use of eye gaze and manual gestures to signal attentional focus and convey labels, and the use of voice to designate and convey" (John L. Locke, *The Child's Path to Spoken Language* [Cambridge, MA: Harvard University Press, 1993], 107 [emphasis in original]). Elsewhere Locke points out that infants who do not find this emotional responsiveness in their mothers seek it from others. Ibid., 109–10.

condition of our respect for them, we can say that our loving infants is part of the process by which infants develop into worthy objects of respect.

Love is respect's pioneer. It goes on ahead and prepares the soil where respect will take root. Respect is what infants will get once they qualify for full membership in the human moral community, but love is what reaches out and brings them into that community and necessarily does so before they qualify. And this love is not compatible with treating infants as expendable, as "trial babies" who may or may not be kept. The love of infants must be genuine and must start early to do its work, and that in turn implies that the naturalness of this love counts toward its goodness.

This gives us enough to characterize the special status that infants have as natural objects of adults' love. As I suggested earlier, love cherishes the sheer existence of its object. Thus, love makes us want very much to protect existing infants and to make sure that they survive. On the other hand, since love is given rather than deserved, it is not based on anything that makes the infants worthy of it. Thus, we find ourselves strongly inclined to believe that it is wrong to kill infants, yet unable to point to some property of infants (not shared by human fetuses, or even by animals that many people think may be acceptably killed) that justifies this belief.

If this is correct, then we can say that the strong belief in the wrongness of killing infants is the product of our natural love for them, coupled with (or strengthened by) our respect for our fellows' love of them. And this love is worth supporting because it is respect's pioneer. By loving infants, we treat them as asymmetrically valuable before they really deserve it, but as part of the process by which they come really to deserve it. Then, it is wrong to kill infants because it is wrong generally to block or frustrate this love for two reasons: (1) because we and our fellows naturally and virtually universally feel this love, and (2) because it is good that we feel it inasmuch as it is important to infants' development into children and adults worthy of respect.

Insofar as respect is a valuation of other people's valuing, we can say that we protect infants out of respect, not for them, but for those who love them. We value that those people—just about everyone—get what they value. And we are supported in this by the general goodness of the love that just about everyone has for infants.

This will not apply to fetuses. They may be objects of love, but not of such love as can play a role in their psychomoral development. That requires a real, interactive social relation that can occur only after birth. Except for the pregnant woman herself, anyone who loves the fetus inside a woman's uterus is loving the object of his imagination, not a being with whom he has interacted. Though this may be an extension of our natural love for infants, it is not the spontaneous emotion itself that became part of us as a result of natural selection. Thus it lacks the warrant of naturalness and virtual universality that characterizes the love of infants. More importantly, since it cannot contribute to the psychomoral development of the fetus, it lacks the warrant of goodness that characterizes the love of infants. This is not to say that the fact that many people love fetuses counts for nothing. Much as respect for our fellows' love for infants justifies protecting infants' lives, I think that respect for those who love fetuses calls for treating aborted fetuses with special care. But, since this is a matter of other people's love rather than fetuses' own worthiness for respect, it surely will not be enough to justify requiring women to stay pregnant against their wills. What I say later about autonomy rights will provide yet further support for this conclusion.

This account denies that the reasons that make it wrong to kill infants are the same as those that make it wrong to kill children or adults. Quite the contrary. Killing children or adults is wrong because it violates the respect they are due as creatures aware of, and caring about, their lives; killing infants, because it violates the love we give them as a means of making them into creatures aware of, and caring about, their lives. Killing children or adults is wrong because of properties *they* possess; killing infants, because of an emotion that *we* naturally and rightly have toward infants. Infants, for the moment, do not possess in their own right a property that makes it wrong to kill them. For this reason, there will be permissible exceptions to the rule against killing them that will not apply to the rule against killing adults or children. In particular, I think (as do many philosophers, doctors, and parents) that ending the lives of severely handicapped newborns will be acceptable. It does not take from the newborns a life that they yet care about, and it is arguably compatible with, rather than violative of, our natural love for infants. Other than that room should be left for the possibility of such exceptions, my argument is compatible with the idea that *legally* we ought to protect infants from being killed by including them under the same laws against homicide that protect children and adults. Nonetheless, my argument does imply that killing infants is not, morally speaking, murder.

The Stages of Human Being and the Ways We Value Life

In *Abortion and Unborn Human Life*, Patrick Lee writes, "To determine whether killing unborn human organisms is wrong, one need only determine what feature of killing adult human organisms makes doing so wrong, and then determine whether that feature is also present in the killing of unborn human organisms."[21] Don Marquis assumes, in effect, the appropriateness of this same methodological approach. However, I have argued that what makes killing infants wrong is different from what makes killing children and adults wrong. And that is enough to show that it cannot be simply assumed, without argument, that the same thing makes the killing of humans wrong whenever it is wrong. I want now to extend this notion and suggest that there are a variety of ways in which we value life and that each has its own ground and its own particular moral implications.

Consider first what I have referred to as the *objectively* good properties of human beings, properties that make the world a better place than it would be without them. Such objectively good properties are symmetrically valuable. That human beings possess such objectively good properties as rationality or capacity for joy and attachment cannot explain the serious wrongness of killing humans, because contraception and abstinence also cause the nonexistence of these good properties. However, this does not imply that these properties play no role in our valuation of human life. On the contrary, they are objects of *categorical* valuing of human life, grounds of our *wanting* human life to go on. Such valuing can be the basis of a general obligation to continue the human race, to husband the earth's resources rather than to squander them, and so on. Though I do not argue for it here, I think that there is such an obligation.[22] However, this obligation does not protect any particular individual, because all that it asks of us is that there continue to exist a substantial, perhaps an optimal, number of human beings. And that in itself is compatible with killing some and replacing them. Nonetheless, this is surely one of the ways in which we value human life.

I have suggested further that the protection we afford to infants is based on the love that human beings naturally have for them. And that this is a weaker basis for protection of infants' lives than for the protection of the lives of children or adults, precisely because it is a matter of other people's love for them, rather than of their care for their own lives. The loss to other people of the object of their love is a lesser loss than the loss to the individual of his own life. The others will live on to love again. The individual who loses his own life will not. On these

---

21. Patrick Lee, *Abortion and Unborn Human Life* (Washington, DC: Catholic University of America Press, 1996), 44.
22. I have argued for such an obligation in my *Justice and Modern Moral Philosophy* (New Haven, CT: Yale University Press, 1990), 184–87.

grounds, I take it that there can be exceptions to the rule against killing infants that would not be justifiable in the case of children or adults. In particular, I think it will be permissible to end the lives of severely defective newborns, though it is not at all permissible to end the lives of severely defective children or adults. Here, then, is yet another way in which we value human life, which has its own distinctive moral implications.

Furthermore, many people (besides the women pregnant with them) claim to love fetuses. While this cannot be a strong enough ground to override a woman's autonomy rights, which are rooted in her awareness and caring about her own life, this love is nonetheless worthy of our respect. We show that respect by according special treatment to fetuses as far as is compatible with respecting the pregnant woman's rights. So, for example, we are rightly careful about how we treat aborted fetuses, how we dispose of them, and so forth. Moreover, while fetuses might legitimately be used for medical purposes that promise great benefits for human children and adults, they should not be used frivolously. Here too is a distinctive way in which to value human life.

The full moral right to protection of one's life becomes appropriate at the point at which the infant starts to be aware of its own life stretching out before it, starts to be aware of itself as the same being at different times, and starts, of course, to be attached to that life—or, perhaps, more precisely, starts to attach its instinctual self-preservative urges to the life of which it has become aware. But note that this is a threshold point. It is the first step, not the last one. Having identified this property as the ground of the full moral right to protection of life, I do not assume that that same property is the one and only property that justifies the protection of human life throughout all of a life's course.

To see how the property that justifies protection changes over time, we follow the same clue that has guided our argument from the beginning; namely, we look at the kind of protection of life that we think appropriate to human beings. The nature of this protection changes as children mature. We start by protecting their lives as such (even, for example, against their own unwise choices), and we evolve in the direction of protecting their ability to make of their lives what they choose. *We move from protecting children's security toward protecting adults' autonomy.* This evolution of protection is appropriate precisely because children's attitude toward their lives evolves as well. They start off with little more than a blind attachment to the lives that they are dimly aware of as theirs. But, as they mature, they come to view their lives, not just as the object of a desire to go on, but as the arena in which they will make their lives what they will be. As their self-awareness deepens to encompass recognition of themselves as having desires, recognition of the world as a place that does not dependably satisfy all their desires, and recognition of their mortality as an outer limit to living the life that is the object of their desires, human beings, I contend, change from beings who simply care blindly about their lives to beings who (normally also, but sometimes instead) experience their lives as the theater of their own happening, the stage upon which is played out the drama of their one and only attempt to live the life they want to live. In response to this change, it is appropriate that our protection changes from protection of humans' lives to protection of their ability to make of their lives what they wish—which necessarily includes protection of their lives, since unchosen death clearly frustrates people's ability to make of their lives what they want. Thus we appropriately grant people autonomy rights, which include their right to protection of their lives. And this is yet another way in which we value human life.

Here my analysis links up with some observations commonly made by existentialists who hold that human beings are beings whose being is "at stake" in their being. By this is meant that humans do not simply live out a predetermined script; they must choose the kind of human being they will be, and their lives are the arena in which this project—whose success is by no means guaranteed—is ventured. As a result of this very fact, Martin Heidegger goes so far as to characterize human being as "care": "Human being is an entity for which, in its being, that being is an issue," and, consequently, human being is "an entity whose being must be defined as 'care.' "[23] This suggests that the quality of experiencing ourselves as "at stake" in our lives is a development of, and out of, the less nuanced attachment to our lives that characterized us as young children.

Most importantly, Heidegger points to the fact that we are still talking about a way in which human beings' lives are subjectively valued by them. And this gives us a way of understanding the way we value people's autonomy as a form of asymmetric valuing: We can value that people who experience themselves as "at stake" in their lives get to make of their lives what they want, without having to value that there be or come into existence people who so experience themselves.

We have here a case of that indirect valuing that I have called respect. Indeed, valuing that people be able to make of their lives what they want is probably the paradigmatic case of respect. But, notice that this respect does not depend on people's wanting to live. Rather, we respect them in a way that treats their lives as theirs to do with what

---

23. Martin Heidegger, *Being and Time* (New York: Harper & Row, 1962), 236–38; see also Reiman, *Justice and Modern Moral Philosophy*, 44.

they want, including (at least for liberals like me) their right to end their lives should they so choose.

For this reason, my argument is not vulnerable to a criticism that Don Marquis has leveled, which may also have occurred to some readers: "If what makes killing us wrong is that we care about our future lives, then because suicidal teenagers, some of the clinically depressed, and some of the brainwashed don't care about the continuation of their lives, killing them is morally permissible."[24] This objection appears to have considerable force until one realizes that it assumes that there is one and only one continuing reason for the (asymmetric) wrongness of killing us. Once this much is clear, the answer to Marquis's objection is that depressed or suicidal teens, as well as brainwashed adults, have *autonomy* rights that entitle them to protection of their lives even if they have stopped caring positively about going on living. So we protect depressed and suicidal teens because we believe that their lives are theirs to make of what they wish—and we try to treat their psychological problems precisely because such problems undermine their ability to live the lives they want. As for victims of brainwashing, their autonomy rights have already been violated by the brainwashing, and that can surely not justify depriving them of the rights (which they can exercise or which others can exercise in their name) that they would have had without the brainwashing.

I think that much the same will apply to the severely retarded and people with senility or Alzheimer's disease. For the most part, such people have the minimum rationality needed for them to still have autonomy rights. Where individuals fall below this minimum, however, I think our attitude toward them shifts back to an attitude analogous to that toward infants. The severely retarded and victims of senility or Alzheimer's are still objects of normal human fellow-feeling—Hume's sentiment of humanity. If some individuals fall below the threshold for having a full moral right to protection based on their rationality, they remain the objects of a normal and virtually universal human affection, which itself is worthy of respect. As with infants, such respect will lead to a strong rule against killing, but a rule that allows exceptions not allowed for normal children and adults. So, for example, if we learn that the life of very advanced Alzheimer's patients is unrelieved suffering, this may justify euthanasia in terms similar to those that justify infanticide of severely defective newborns. And, as in the case of infanticide, while laws should leave room for this possibility, we should still *legally* protect the lives of the severely retarded, the senile

---

24. Don Marquis, "Reiman on Abortion," *Journal of Social Philosophy* 29, no. 1 (Spring 1998): 143.

and the victims of Alzheimer's, by including them under the same law against homicide that protects normal children and adults. Here, then, we have yet another way in which to value human life.

Finally, I think that, just as respect for the love that people have toward fetuses calls for special care in treating and disposing of aborted fetuses, so the love that human beings have for their fellows calls for special care in the treating and disposing of human corpses. And this too is a way in which we value human life.

Abortion and Liberal Discourse

In his important book *Political Liberalism*, Harvard philosopher John Rawls has argued that there are limits on the kinds of reasons that can be used to justify laws and policies in a liberal state. Rawls has called political discourse that is subject to these limits "public reason." The idea is that "citizens are to conduct their public political discussions of constitutional essentials and matters of basic justice within the framework of what each sincerely regards as a reasonable political conception of justice, a conception that expresses political values that others as free and equal also might reasonably be expected reasonably to endorse."[25] Rawls presents a design for a politically liberal society in which people with differing moral and theological views can form a moral consensus about the guiding values of their shared political existence. Hence his conception of public discourse is governed by the idea of reciprocity, according to which, arguments about public legal measures are to be made in terms that each believes the others, though differing in their moral and theological views, can accept.

Rawls characterizes his liberalism as "political" to distinguish it from liberalism that is based on a comprehensive moral or metaphysical or religious doctrine and that, as a result, puts itself forth as true for all, regardless of their personal moral and theological views. My own view of liberalism is not what Rawls would call "political." Rather it is based squarely on a comprehensive moral doctrine. I have argued elsewhere that living according to one's own choices and judgments is a necessary condition of living a good life.[26] For this reason, plus the fact that preserving freedom allows people of all different beliefs to

25. John Rawls, *Political Liberalism* (New York: Columbia University Press, 1993), 212–54. Rawls has clarified and modified his conception of public reason in the introduction to the paperback edition of *Political Liberalism* (New York: Columbia University Press, 1996), l–lvii (quotation from paperback ed., p. l).

26. See Jeffrey Reiman, *Critical Moral Liberalism: Theory and Practice* (Lanham, MD: Rowman & Littlefield, 1997), 16–18.

live together peacefully, I contend that there is a moral obligation to comply with the principles of liberalism that is based on reasons that override individuals' personal moral and theological views. Consequently, while I agree with Rawls that there are appropriate limits on the terms of liberal political discourse, I think that they need to be stated more specifically than he does, and that they must be shown more clearly to relate to the moral ideal of liberalism. In this final section, I want to sketch briefly the conception of the limits of liberal political discourse that follows from my view of liberalism and show how the argument that I have given here about abortion and the various ways we value human life occurs within these appropriate limits.

Because of its commitment to the overriding goodness of freedom, a liberal society promotes and protects the possibility of people living lives based on their own choices and judgments. Consequently, the most important liberal principles are those that specify the conditions under which coercion can be justified. And these principles rule out certain considerations from being used to justify coercion. Thus they specify a special mode of political discourse, which I call *liberal discourse*. The shape of this discourse is given by two general principles, which I call the *principle of subjective preference* and the *principle of individual priority*. Note that these principles apply only to public discussions that aim at justifying the use of coercion. In all other areas, at least among adults, a liberal society tolerates no substantive limits on the terms of discourse.

The principle of subjective preference holds that arguments should be made in terms of what people want to have or to avoid (under which I include what they choose for or against and what they value or disvalue, plus whatever is needed for people to identify their true wants), rather than in terms of what has intrinsic value. The principle does not deny that some things have intrinsic value; it merely rules out appeal to such value for the purpose of arguments about the use of public force (which includes the use of public funds, since these are obtained by the threat and use of force). One should not overestimate how much will be ruled out by the principle of subjective preference, since most things that are plausible candidates for intrinsic value are also wanted by people (say, great paintings or beautiful natural settings) or are part of background conditions (such as education or free expression) that enable people to identify what they truly want. The reason for the principle of subjective preference is that an appeal to intrinsic value that does not correspond to what people themselves want risks imposing (that is, forcing) others' judgments on them, whereas liberalism is committed to maximizing their ability to make their lives the outcome of their own judgments.

The principle of individual priority holds that what a person wants for himself has a very strong presumption over what any number of others want for him. Here, too, it should be obvious how this principle supports the liberal attempt to promote freedom and limit the use of force.

The principles of subjective value and individual priority yield a distinction between primary and secondary value. *Primary value* is that bestowed upon something desired by an individual for himself, and *secondary value* is that bestowed upon something desired by someone for someone else. Because of the primacy of individual freedom, a liberal society is committed to almost never allowing secondary value—no matter how many people desire it—to trump primary value. I say almost never, since there may be situations where a very widely and strongly desired secondary value might prevail over a narrowly and weakly desired primary value. For example, the desire of some to walk around in the nude or to exhibit obscene pictures or signs might be limited in light of the desire of others not to have to see such things. The liberal solution to such problems normally takes the form of some sort of zoning compromise, in which a limited area (nudist colonies, red-light zones) is set aside to permit the unpopular activity to exist for those who desire it, while leaving the others able not to have to see it.

The grounds for the asymmetric value of human life conform to the principles of liberal discourse—or, as I would prefer to believe, here our valuation of human life shows its deep liberal roots. This is so both negatively and positively. Negatively, we have seen that asymmetric value cannot be grounded on the intrinsic value of human life, since, aside from the difficulty of establishing its existence, such value is present in all humans—existing and future ones—and thus cannot account for asymmetry. Positively, what can account for asymmetric value is the actual caring about a life, either by the one whose life it is or by others. Thus this value can be accounted for within the limits of the principle of subjective preference. In addition, the protection of infants, the severely retarded, and the senile, as well as the respectful treatment of aborted fetuses and corpses, depends, in my view, on what people actually desire, and thus it, too, is accounted for within the limits of the principle of subjective preference. Moreover, that this latter protection is weaker than that accorded to beings who care about their own lives, and weaker than a woman's right to control her body, conforms to the principle of individual priority. A child's or adult's right to protection of her life, as well as a woman's right to control her body, are primary values since they are rooted in the concerned individual's preferences for herself. The rights of fetuses, infants, the severely retarded, and the senile, as well as restrictions on the treatment of aborted fetuses and human corpses generally, are secondary values, since they are rooted in the preferences of others.

The argument I have given in this book is a distinctively liberal one, not only in the obvious sense that it dovetails with what is called a liberal position on abortion, but also in the important sense that it complies with defensible limits on the kinds of reasons that can be used to justify coercion in a liberal state. Indeed, here my argument comes full circle, since the limited defense I offered in chapter 1 for the Supreme Court's decision in *Roe v. Wade* can be understood now as showing how the decision conforms to the principles of liberal discourse. The idea that controversial theories of the life, status, or personhood of the fetus should not be enforced finds support in the principle of subjective preference. The idea that a woman should be able to decide for herself whether to continue a pregnancy—rather than be subject to the community's views about this, or to its ideas about womanhood or sexuality—corresponds to the principle of individual priority.

To be sure, this does not mean that all citizens of a liberal state, including those with deep religious objections to abortion, will find my argument in this book, or Justice Blackmun's in *Roe v. Wade, reasonable* according to their overall moral or theological doctrines. Rather, liberalism enables us to say to such people and others: Whether or not you think this is reasonable according to your basic moral or theological views, the goodness of the life protected for you by liberalism obligates you to comply with its outcome.

Index

About the Author

Jeffrey Reiman is William Fraser McDowell Professor of Philosophy at American University in Washington, D.C. Born in Brooklyn, New York, in 1942, Reiman received his B.A. in Philosophy from Queens College in 1963 and his Ph.D. in Philosophy from Pennsylvania State University in 1968. He was a Fulbright Scholar in India during 1966–67.

Reiman joined the American University faculty in 1970, in the Center for the Administration of Justice (now called the Department of Justice, Law and Society of the School of Public Affairs). After several years of holding a joint appointment in the Justice program and the Department of Philosophy and Religion, he joined the Department of Philosophy and Religion full-time in 1988, becoming director of the Master's Program in Philosophy and Social Policy. He was named William Fraser McDowell Professor of Philosophy in 1990.

Reiman is a member of the Phi Beta Kappa and Phi Kappa Phi honor societies, and past president of the American University Phi Beta Kappa chapter. He is the author of *In Defense of Political Philosophy* (Harper & Row, 1972), *Justice and Modern Moral Philosophy* (Yale University Press, 1990), *Critical Moral Liberalism: Theory and Practice* (Rowman & Littlefield, 1997), *The Rich Get Richer and the Poor Get Prison: Ideology, Class, and Criminal Justice,* 5th edition (Allyn & Bacon, 1998), *The Death Penalty: For and Against* (with Louis P. Pojman) (Rowman & Littlefield, 1998), and more than fifty articles in philosophy and criminal justice journals and anthologies.